W9-APX-011

Rhythm Reading

second edition

Rhythm Reading

Elementary through Advanced Training

Daniel Kazez

W. W. NORTON & COMPANY
NEW YORK   LONDON

Copyright © 1997 by W. W. Norton & Company, Inc. Copyright ©
1989 by Daniel Kazez

All Rights Reserved
Printed in the United States of America

The text of this book is composed in Garamond.
with the display set in Matrix.
Composition by Music By Design, Inc.
Manufacturing by Kingsport Press.
Book design by Maura Fadden Rosenthal / Mspace.
Cover illustration: SURVAGE, Léopold. *Color Rhythm.* One of fifty-nine
              studies for the film. (1913) 13 x 12 1/4" (33 x 31.1
              cm). Watercolor, and brush and ink on paper, The
              Museum of Modern Art, New York. Purchase.
              Photograph © 1996 The Museum of Modern Art,
              New York.

Library of Congress Cataloging-in-Publication Data

Kazez, Daniel.
    Rhythm reading: elementary through advanced training / Daniel
Kazez.—2nd ed.
        p.   cm.
    Includes bibliographical references and index.
    ISBN 0-393-97073-6
    1. Musical meter and rhythm—Studies and exercises.   2. Sight-
reading (Music)   I. Title.
MT42.K3   1997
781.2´2—dc20   96-21128

Since this page cannot legibly accommodate all the copyright notices,
pages 225–26 constitute an extension of the copyright page.

W. W. Norton & Company, Inc., 500 Fifth Avenue, New York, N.Y. 10110
              http://www.wwnorton.com

W. W. Norton & Company Ltd., 10 Coptic Street, London WC1A 1PU

6 7 8 9 0

TO RE (A.K.), L.j. (B.K.), AND R.K.

I got rhythm...
—IRA GERSHWIN

Rhythm and motion...
are the foundations of musical art.
—IGOR STRAVINSKY

CONTENTS

Preface xv

Introduction 1
Rhythm and Pitch 1
Hints for Practicing 1
Conducting 2
Tempo Markings 3

UNIT I FUNDAMENTAL RHYTHM PATTERNS 5

Chapter 1 Simple Meter 7

Simple and Compound Meters 7
Time Signatures for Simple Meters 8
Simple Duple, Triple, and Quadruple Meters with a Quarter-Note Beat 9

Exercises 10
Quadruple meter • Half rest • Tie • Note endings • Duple meter • Triple meter • Augmentation dot • Whole note and whole-note rest • Beaming • Common time • Whole-measure rest • Meter changes • Composite meters • Conducting in ⁵₄ (2+3) • Conducting in ⁵₄ (3+2) • Conducting in ⁷₄ • Canon • Hocket

Self-Test on Written Concepts 24
Recommended Listening 26

Chapter 2 Compound Meter 28

Time Signatures for Compound Meters 28
Compound Duple, Triple, and Quadruple Meters with a Dotted Quarter-
    Note Beat 31

Exercises 31
One beat per measure • Beaming over rests • The ⁄. sign • Retrograde canon

Self-Test on Written Concepts 40
Recommended Listening 41

Chapter 3   Simple Meter: Quarter-Note Beat   42

Exercises   42
*Anacrusis • Multi-measure rests • Inverted dotting • Double dotting •
Measured tremolo • Augmentation canon*

Self-Test on Written Concepts   55

Chapter 4   Compound Meter: Dotted Quarter-Note Beat   57

Exercises   57
One beat per measure • Measured tremolo • Split measures

Self-Test on Written Concepts   66

Chapter 5   Simple Meter: Half-Note Beat   67

Equivalent Cells   67

Exercises   68
Double whole note; double whole rest • Alla breve • Hypermeter • Diminution canon

Self-Test on Written Concepts   79

Chapter 6   Compound Meter: Dotted Half-Note Beat   80

Equivalent Cells   80

Exercises   81
Hypermeter

Self-Test on Written Concepts   90

Chapter 7   Simple Meter: Eighth-Note Beat   91

Equivalent Cells   91

Exercises   92
♪ = ♪

Self-Test on Written Concepts   100

Chapter 8 Compound Meter: Dotted Eighth-Note Beat 101

Equivalent Cells 101

Exercises 102

Self-Test on Written Concepts 108

UNIT II IRREGULAR DIVISION OF THE BEAT 109

Chapter 9 Simple Meter: All Beat Values 111

Introduction to Irregular Division of the Beat 111
Quarter-Note Beat 113

Exercises 113
Triplets • Quintuplets • Sextuplets • Septuplets • Irregular division with measured tremolo

Half-Note Beat 120

Exercises 121

Eighth-Note Beat 123

Exercises 123

Self-Test on Written Concepts 125

Chapter 10 Compound Meter: All Beat Values 127

Irregular Division of the Beat in Compound Meter 127
Dotted Quarter-Note Beat 128

Exercises 128
Duplets • Quadruplets • Quintuplets • Septuplets

Dotted Half-Note Beat 132

Exercises 133

Dotted Eighth-Note Beat 136

Exercises 137

Self-Test on Written Concepts 138

UNIT III   SYNCOPATION   141

Chapter 11   Simple Meter: Quarter-Note Beat   143

Introduction to Syncopation   143

Exercises   145
*Cross rhythms: superduplet • Supertriplet • Less common cross rhythms •
"Four against three" • "Three against four" • "Two against five"*

Self-Test on Written Concepts   154
Recommended Listening   155

Chapter 12   Compound Meter: All Beat Values   156

Dotted Quarter-Note Beat   156

Exercises   156
Hemiola

Dotted Half-Note Beat   160

Exercises   160

Dotted Eighth-Note Beat   162

Exercises   162

Self-Test on Written Concepts   165

Chapter 13   Simple Meter: Half-Note Beat; Eighth-Note Beat   167

Half-Note Beat   167

Exercises   168

Eighth-Note Beat   174

Exercises   174

Self-Test on Written Concepts   180

UNIT IV   EXCERPTS FROM MUSIC LITERATURE   183

Chapter 14   Excerpts in Traditional Meters   185
Exercises   185
Rhythmic alteration in Baroque music

Chapter 15   More Challenging Excerpts in Traditional Meters   193
Exercises   193

Chapter 16   Excerpts in Nontraditional Meters   203
Composite Meter   203
Exercises   204
Double Meter   208
Exercises   208
Unusual Beat Units   209
Exercises   209
Longa
Metric Modulation   210
Exercises   211
Polymetric Music   212
Exercises   212
Ametric Music   213
Exercises   214
Self-Test on Written Concepts   216

Appendix A   Special Rhythmic Symbols in Twentieth-Century Music   217

Appendix B   Rhythm Cells   219
Simple Meter   219
Compound Meter   220

Appendix C   Recommended Speech Cues   221
Simple Meter   221
Compound Meter   222

Glossary of Musical Terms   223

Acknowledgments   225

Index   227

PREFACE

Overview

Rhythm Reading: Elementary through Advanced Training is a comprehensive study of the rhythm patterns students are likely to encounter when playing, singing, conducting, teaching, composing, or studying music. It is designed to be used in college-level sight singing classes. It is expected that students using this book will have at least a rudimentary knowledge of music reading.

Rhythm Reading contains pure rhythm exercises composed by the author, as well as excerpts from music literature. The styles of all periods of music history are included, medieval through modern. Students sing, tap, or play the exercises while conducting, tapping, or counting the beat. For coordination, *Rhythm Reading* includes two-part exercises in which each student performs both parts simultaneously. The ensemble exercises (duets and trios) are ideal for performance by the class as a whole or by a few selected students. These exercises feature such compositional techniques as canon, augmentation, diminution, and hocket.

Organization of the text

Rhythm Reading is divided into four units:

Unit I, "Fundamental Rhythm Patterns," introduces the rhythm patterns that occur most frequently in Western music.

Unit II, "Irregular Division of the Beat," includes simple-meter exercises that use triplets and sextuplets and compound-meter exercises that use duplets and quadruplets. Quintuplets and septuplets are introduced in both meters.

Unit III, "Syncopation," includes the following rhythm patterns, among others:

$$\frac{2}{4}\ \eighth\ \quarter\qquad\eighth\ \|\ \frac{2}{4}\ \quarter\ \quarter\ \quarter\underbracket{\ \ }_{3}\ \|\ \frac{3}{4}\ \half\ \half\underbracket{\ \ }_{2}\ \|\ \frac{6}{8}\ \quarter\ \quarter\ \quarter\ \|$$

Unit IV, "Excerpts from Music Literature," features music in such commonly used meters as $\frac{3}{4}$ and $\frac{6}{8}$ as well as in unusual meters such as $\frac{3}{1}$, $\frac{3}{32}$, and $\frac{10}{16}$. Chapters 14 and 15 present these excerpts in a graded sequence; Chapter 16 offers excerpts in composite meter and double meter, and introduces metric modulation, polymetric music, and ametric music.

Organization within chapters

Most chapters in *Rhythm Reading* have the following sections:

- One-part exercises.

- More challenging one-part exercises, based on material presented earlier in the chapter.

- Two-part exercises for one person, to improve the student's ability to follow two lines simultaneously.

- Ensemble exercises for more than one person.

- Review exercises, using meters and rhythm material from previous chapters.

- Self-tests on written concepts. These written questions address each major concept covered in the chapter and give students the opportunity to write their own exercises using the cells and meters that have been introduced.

Function and pedagogical approach

The primary function of *Rhythm Reading* is to improve students' rhythm skills. This is accomplished by studying and performing a series of carefully graded exercises. Each chapter is devoted to either simple meters or compound meters. In simple meter, the following beat values are used: quarter note (e.g., $\frac{2}{4}$, $\frac{3}{4}$, $\frac{4}{4}$), half note (e.g., $\frac{2}{2}$, $\frac{3}{2}$, $\frac{4}{2}$), and eighth note (e.g., $\frac{2}{8}$, $\frac{3}{8}$, $\frac{4}{8}$). In compound meter, the following beat values are used: dotted quarter note (e.g., $\frac{6}{8}$, $\frac{9}{8}$, $\frac{12}{8}$), dotted half note (e.g., $\frac{6}{4}$, $\frac{9}{4}$, $\frac{12}{4}$), and dotted eighth note (e.g., $\frac{6}{16}$, $\frac{9}{16}$, $\frac{12}{16}$).

Students learn to read rhythm not as individual notes but as groups of notes, which are presented in this text as "rhythm cells."* Each exercise teaches a new cell or reviews cells that have already been learned. Each cell is introduced in a meter with a quarter-note beat (e.g., $\frac{2}{4}$) or a dotted quarter-note beat (e.g., $\frac{6}{8}$) and is displayed in a box with an "**x**" indicating the location of the beat. For example,

Before a new rhythm cell appears in a full-length exercise, it usually appears in a short preparatory drill. Some of the drills prepare the student for the cell by showing (through notation and performance) that the cell can be thought of in terms of a previously learned cell, as illustrated below. (Horizontal brackets under notes indicate rhythm patterns that sound the same but are notated differently.)

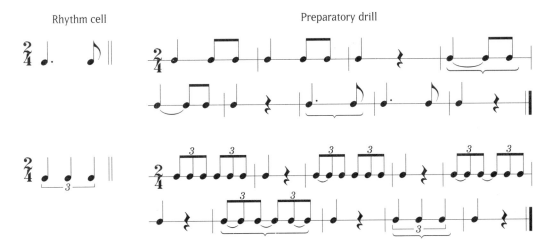

Other preparatory drills prepare students for a cell through repetition:

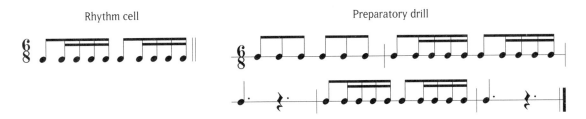

Several pages or chapters later, each cell appears again as an equivalent cell in a related meter. For example,

*A complete list of these cells, in all meters, appears in Appendix B. A detailed discussion of teaching with rhythm cells may be found in John D. White, *Guidelines for College Teaching of Music Theory* (Metuchen, N.J.: Scarecrow Press, 1981), pp. 38–39.

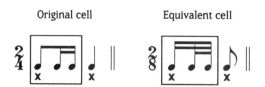

To help students understand that a rhythm cell in a given meter can be transformed into an equivalent cell in a different meter, many chapters include worksheets in which students rewrite previously learned rhythm cells using a meter with a different beat unit.

Throughout *Rhythm Reading*, cells appear in many permutations, for example, with ties added or with notes of the cell replaced with rests:

Spiral learning is accomplished because each rhythm cell (both in its original form and in new versions) reappears at regular intervals throughout the book.

In addition to performance, *Rhythm Reading* provides students with a thorough understanding of the essential elements of rhythm and meter, such as simple and compound meter, irregular division of the beat, syncopation, composite meter, and hemiola. To this end, the text includes explanations, illustrations, and etymologies of important terms and concepts. In many cases, students are provided with immediate practice in applying this material in brief worksheets. In addition, many folk songs and excerpts from the classical music repertory are included as illustrations. For all folk songs, a key and starting pitch are suggested to help ensure successful in-class performance.

Recommended teaching methods

The following teaching methods are particularly effective with this text:

- **Speech cue method:** Researchers in rhythm pedagogy have demonstrated that students learn rhythm more easily and accurately when using a "speech cue method."* Here, a rhythm cell is learned not on a fixed syllable (such as "ta") but on a carefully selected word. The word chosen must fit the cell in relative syllable lengths and accents. The following rhythm, for example, might be learned with the word "telephone":

*See, for example, Muriel J. Bebeau, "Effects of Traditional and Simplified Methods of Rhythm-Reading Instruction," *Journal of Research in Music Education* 30 (1982): 107–19.

Speech cues have been an extremely successful tool in helping students master the rhythmic component of music. A complete list of the speech cues suggested for use in this text appears in Appendix B.*

• **Echoing:** Music educators such as Carl Orff and Zoltán Kodály have suggested that just as children learn to read only after they can speak, students should read music only after they can sing or play an instrument proficiently. "Much musical experience precedes symbolization. The teaching order is always sound to sight, concrete to abstract."† This concept can be incorporated into a sight singing class for introducing especially difficult rhythm cells. Before students perform exercises incorporating such a cell, they can mimic the professor as he or she sings the cell or the preparatory drill used to introduce it.

• **Preview:** For individual exercises, examine potential performing problems and solutions. In class, students should learn *how* to practice, not just *what* to practice.

• **Buddy system:** Students should be encouraged to practice the exercises using the "buddy system": In pairs, students can perform for each other out of class. The student who listens to a partner temporarily assumes the role of teacher. Both students benefit from this type of practice.

• **Rhythm dictation:** Students will learn to *perform* rhythm if they learn to *hear* rhythm. The professor can create short, simple rhythm dictation exercises that incorporate new cells as they are introduced in the text. The process of hearing, identifying, and notating rhythm helps students better understand and perform rhythm.

• **Sing back:** Rhythm cells and speech cues should be reviewed regularly. In my classes, as an extension of dictation, I sing two or three cells in succession (on the syllable "ta"); my students then sing the rhythm back with speech cues, as illustrated below.

Then, immediately, I sing a new measure, continuing the process until students can respond accurately and effortlessly.

---

*In addition to the speech cue method, the professor may choose from several other successful systems that use rhythm syllables:

    Kodály: Lois Chosky, *The Kodály Context: Creating an Environment for Musical Learning* (Englewood Cliffs, N.J.: Prentice-Hall, 1981);

    Gordon: Edwin E. Gordon, *Learning Sequences in Music* (Chicago: GIA Publications, 1983);

    Takadimi: Richard M. Hoffman, William L. Pelto, and John W. White, "Takadimi: A Beat-Oriented System of Rhythm Pedagogy," *Journal of Music Theory Pedagogy* 10 (1996).

†Chosky, *The Kodály Context,* p. 10.

Sequence of chapters

Within each unit, the chapters may be presented in any order, provided that those devoted to the quarter-note beat (e.g., in Unit I, Chapters 1 and 3) and dotted quarter-note beat (e.g., in Unit I, Chapters 2 and 4) are presented first. After covering the material in Chapter 1, for example, one may wish to proceed to Chapter 2, which presents new material in compound meter; to Chapter 3, which is basically a continuation of Chapter 1; or even to the first half of Chapters 5 or 7, both of which offer similar material in simple meters with a half-note beat and eighth-note beat.

After completing Chapters 1–4, one may proceed to Chapters 5, 6, 7, or 8, each of which presents material similar to that in the first four chapters but with different beat units. One may also proceed directly to Unit II—in particular, to the first section of Chapters 9 or 10—before covering the later chapters in Unit I.

If a chapter is presented out of order, or if it is omitted entirely, it may be best to avoid assigning later review exercises that refer to that chapter. (Review exercises appear at the end of every chapter except Chapter 1.)

How to perform the exercises

Using *Rhythm Reading* in classes over the years, I have discovered many possible ways to have my students perform the exercises. In addition to my own experience, many users of the book (professors and students alike) have shared with me their ideas for in-class and out-of-class performance. Here are many of these performance options.

PERFORMING THE RHYTHM

The rhythm in each exercise may be performed in many different ways:

- Sing "ta." (This is probably the best method.) The entire class sings a single pitch; or, better yet, the class is divided into two or more sections and each section sings a different pitch.

- Sing using the speech cue for a rhythm cell just introduced, but sing "ta" for all other notes. Use this system only for the preparatory exercise that introduces a new rhythm cell and for one full-length exercise.

- Sing nonsense syllables (as in scat singing).

- Sing the alphabet from beginning to end continuously and repeatedly through the exercise.

- Repeat a word or name (of at least two syllables), for example:

• Perform the exercise on a scale. For example, perform

in C major as

• Make no sound at all! "Sing" the rhythm silently.

• Play a musical instrument.

• Tap the rhythm on a table using alternate hands, for example:

• Two students play "pat-a-cake." The students stand or sit face-to-face and alternately clap each other's opposite hands, for example:

• The entire class plays "pat-a-cake." The class sits in a circle and each student claps the rhythm with the neighbor to the left and right at the same time.

• With the class divided into two or more groups, one group sings the exercise and the other group or groups sing any rhythm cell as an ostinato.

• Students perform one measure each, in succession, with no pause between measures.

CHOOSING A PITCH

When choosing a pitch for singing the exercises, the professor may wish to:

• Play a chord on the piano using traditional or non-traditional harmony and let students freely choose one pitch to sing.

• Give no starting pitch or chord. Have students pick any starting pitch. Students then have these further options:

Hold the pitch throughout the exercise.

Change pitch freely.

Change pitch, but adhere to a single scale or mode.

KEEPING TRACK OF THE BEAT

Students may keep track of the beat as follows:

- Conduct. (This method is probably the best.)
- Tap with either hand or with a single finger on either hand.
- Count out loud.
- Tap a foot, walk in tempo, or use a metronome.
- Count the beat silently.

The methods below will help students externalize the meter, as well as the beat.

- Walk one step per beat or walk forward for one measure and backward for the next.
- Hop on each downbeat while tapping the rhythm.
- Move the hands (as a unit) while tapping the rhythm:

    In duple meters (such as $\frac{2}{4}$ and $\frac{6}{8}$), the hands move back and forth:

     .

    In triple meters (such as $\frac{3}{4}$ and $\frac{9}{8}$), the hands move to the points of an imaginary triangle: ▽ .

    In quadruple meters (such as $\frac{4}{4}$ and $\frac{12}{8}$), the hands move in a circle, with beats at 12:00, 3:00, 6:00, and 9:00 on an imaginary clock.

- Tap each note that falls on the beat, using both hands on a table, and clap both hands on all other notes.
- Sing the rhythm on a syllable such as "ta," using a different syllable (such as "tee") for each note that falls on the beat.

TWO-PART EXERCISES FOR ONE PERSON

In the two-part exercises, students may use a combination of singing, tapping, or playing an instrument. For example, they might choose one of the following options:

- Tap each part with a different hand. Use two keys on a piano, or simply tap on a desk or table.
- Tap one part and sing the other.
- Play one part on an instrument and sing the other.

To avoid making the two-part exercises too difficult, dynamics have not been added.

ENSEMBLE EXERCISES

The ensemble exercises are meant to be performed by two or more students. To keep the lines of music distinct, students in class may sing the individual parts on different pitches or on different syllables, such as "tee" and "too."

Acknowledgments

I would like to thank the reviewers of the text for their many excellent recommendations: David Garner, San Francisco Conservatory of Music; Ronald Hemmel, Westminster Choir College of Rider University; and Gary Potter, Indiana University. Further, I extend my gratitude to Stephen Squires, Northern Illinois University, for providing many suggestions for how to perform the exercises in class; Stephen Siek, Wittenberg University, for helping me wrestle with musicological conundrums; and John W. White, Ithaca College, for providing a cogent explanation of the "takadimi" system of rhythm syllables. I offer my deepest thanks to Robert Fleisher, Northern Illinois University, who examined the book cover-to-cover on several occasions and provided me with invaluable suggestions, particularly on matters dealing with twentieth-century rhythmic notation.

I would like to acknowledge my appreciation to the students of my sight singing classes who, over the years, have helped me test, proof, and edit every page of the text. Their constructive criticism has provided me with a steady stream of new ideas. Thanks are also due to my faculty aides, who spent countless hours helping to prepare the manuscript, and to Wittenberg University, which provided financial support at various stages of the project. Suzanne La Plante, my editor at W. W. Norton, read my manuscript with a critical eye, simultaneously speaking for the needs of the student and the professor. She worked tirelessly to shape a manuscript that needed much shaping. My wife, Arlin, was involved in making virtually every major decision regarding this text. I am grateful for her constant support and innumerable suggestions for revisions.

Rhythm Reading

Introduction

Rhythm and pitch

In your lives as musicians, you will play, sing, conduct, teach, compose, or study music. In order to succeed in these endeavors, it is crucial that you acquire the ability to recognize, reproduce, and notate the rhythm and pitch elements of music.

If you glance at the last three chapters of this book (beginning on page 185), you will discover music excerpts of considerable complexity. (In the last three chapters, you will be expected to practice and perform only the rhythm element of these excerpts.) This music appears to consist of an endless array of different rhythm patterns. In fact, virtually every rhythm pattern in this music (as well as nearly all of the music you will encounter as students and professionals) is based on one of a small collection of rhythm "building blocks" known in this book as *rhythm cells*. The fundamental purpose of this book is to help you learn to identify and perform these essential rhythm patterns.

To this end, you will practice and perform a variety of rhythm exercises. In addition, you will learn the meaning of important terms and concepts dealing with rhythm and meter.

Hints for practicing

The key to your success in this course (and in your performance area) is your commitment to regular, consistent, and intelligent practicing. Take the following steps when practicing each exercise:

1. Decide whether the exercise is in simple or compound meter. Find the rhythmic value of one beat. (You will learn how to do this in Chapters 1 and 2.)

2. Identify especially difficult passages. Practice these passages—silently or out loud—at a slow tempo.

3. Find the fastest notes in the exercise. Choose a tempo that is slow enough to allow you to perform these notes correctly and confidently.

4. Practice the first measure or two at the tempo you have chosen.

5. Perform the exercise. Look at least one or two beats ahead as you go.

6. Use a metronome occasionally to help you maintain a steady tempo.

Most important, practice the exercise until you can perform it accurately and confidently, without stopping or hesitating.

Conducting

Conducting is an ideal tool for keeping track of the beat. It is superior to foot tapping, which is noisy, habit forming, and, generally speaking, unacceptable in public performance. Conduct using the patterns below. These patterns will be introduced individually in Chapter 1.

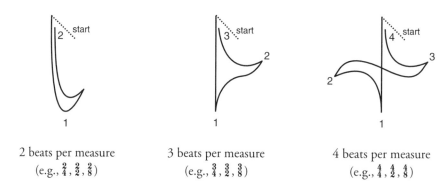

2 beats per measure
(e.g., $\frac{2}{4}, \frac{2}{2}, \frac{2}{8}$) 3 beats per measure
(e.g., $\frac{3}{4}, \frac{3}{2}, \frac{3}{8}$) 4 beats per measure
(e.g., $\frac{4}{4}, \frac{4}{2}, \frac{4}{8}$)

Conduct using a pencil or baton, or simply an empty hand. Practice each pattern until it is second nature. Note that the first beat of each measure is always conducted with a downward gesture; the last beat of each measure is always conducted with an upward gesture. Indicate the exact point of the beat—known as the *ictus*—with a slight flicking gesture. Conduct in a relaxed fashion. Be sure the conducting pattern is neither too large nor too small.

Other conducting patterns appear on pages 19–20 (5 beats per measure) and pages 36–37 (1 beat per measure).

Tempo markings

Below is a summary of the tempo markings included in the exercises.

Adagio	slower
Andante	
Moderato	
Allegretto	
Allegro	
Presto	faster

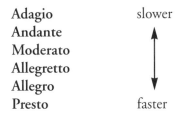

Explanations of musical terms that appear in the excerpts from the literature may be found in the Glossary of Musical Terms at the back of the book.

Fundamental Rhythm Patterns

Simple meter

Simple and compound meters

In music, *meter* refers to the organization or pattern of beats and divisions of the beat. Meter, as indicated by a *time signature* such as $\frac{2}{4}$ or $\frac{6}{8}$, is identified as "simple" or "compound" according to how each beat is divided. In *simple meter*, each beat is usually divided into *two* equal parts. In *compound meter*, each beat is usually divided into *three* equal parts. We will discuss compound meter in detail in Chapter 2.

The song "Twinkle, Twinkle Little Star" is in simple meter. To demonstrate this, you may wish to sing the song in class, with half the class singing the tune and half the class singing a two-syllable word (such as *ba-ker*) on each beat. Notice how well the two parts fit together.

▸ Sing "Twinkle, Twinkle Little Star" (in C major, start on C). Tap the beat (**x**):

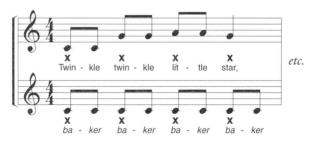

Twinkle, twinkle little star,
How I wonder what you are.
Up above the world so high,
Like a diamond in the sky,
Twinkle, twinkle little star,
How I wonder what you are.

"Over the River and through the Wood" is in compound meter. To demonstrate this, half the class can sing the song while the other half sings a three-syllable word (such as *Bee-tho-ven*) on each beat. Again, notice how well the two parts fit together.

▸ Sing "Over the River and through the Wood" (in C major, start on G). Tap the beat (**x**):

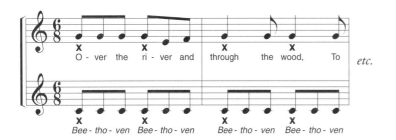

Over the river and through the wood,
To grandmother's house we go;
The horse knows the way to carry the sleigh,
Through white and drifted snow.
Over the river and through the wood,
Oh, how the wind does blow!
It stings the toes and bites the nose,
As over the fields we go!

Worksheet No. 1
Simple and Compound Meters

Sing each song below, and then identify the meter of each as simple or compound. Tap the beat, which is indicated with an "**x**." Does the beat seem to be divided into two parts (simple meter) or three parts (compound meter)?

1. "Jingle Bells" (in E♭ major, start on G), refrain:
   Jin - gle bells, jin - gle bells, jin - gle all the way,...
     x   **x**   **x**   **x**   **x**   **x** **x**

2. "Hickory Dickory Dock" (in C major, start on E):
   Hick - o - ry dick - o ry dock,....
     x   **x**   **x**

3. "The Mulberry Bush" (in E major, start on E):
   Here we go 'round the mul - ber - ry bush,...
     x   **x**   **x**   **x**

4. "Deck the Halls" (in C major, start on G):
   Deck the halls with boughs of hol - ly,...
    x **x**   **x**   **x**   **x**   **x**   **x**

5. "Silent Night" (in A♭ major, start on E♭):
   Si - lent night, Ho - ly night,...
   x   **x**   **x**   **x**

6. "London Bridge" (in D major, start on A):
   Lon - don Bridge is fall - ing down,...
   x   **x**   **x**   **x**

Time signatures for simple meters

In simple meter, the *top* number of the time signature indicates the number of beats in each measure. For example, in $\frac{2}{4}$ each measure contains two beats: $\frac{2}{4}$ ♩ ♩ . In $\frac{3}{4}$, each measure contains three beats: $\frac{3}{4}$ ♩ ♩ ♩ . The *bottom* number in simple meter indicates the type of note (e.g., quarter note or half note) that receives one beat. For example, in $\frac{2}{4}$ the quarter note receives one beat. The quarter note is therefore known as the *beat unit* in $\frac{2}{4}$. In $\frac{2}{2}$, the beat unit is the half note; it receives one beat: $\frac{2}{2}$ ♩ ♩ .

The most frequently used simple meters appear below.

Time signatures	Beat unit	Example
$\frac{2}{4}, \frac{3}{4}, \frac{4}{4}$	♩	$\frac{2}{4}$
$\frac{2}{2}, \frac{3}{2}, \frac{4}{2}$	𝅗𝅥	$\frac{2}{2}$
$\frac{2}{8}, \frac{3}{8}, \frac{4}{8}$	♪	$\frac{2}{8}$

Simple Meter

2 → two beats in each measure
4 → the quarter note is the beat unit

Worksheet No. 2
Simple-Meter Time Signatures

For each of the simple meters listed below, identify the number of beats per measure and the beat unit. Then write one measure of rhythm for each meter.

1. $\frac{2}{4}$ 2. $\frac{3}{4}$ 3. $\frac{4}{8}$ 4. $\frac{7}{2}$

5. $\frac{2}{8}$ 6. $\frac{2}{1}$ 7. $\frac{5}{4}$ 8. $\frac{3}{16}$

Simple duple, triple, and quadruple meters with a quarter-note beat

Simple meters are classified according to the number of beats per measure: *Duple meter* (e.g., $\frac{2}{4}$, $\frac{2}{2}$, $\frac{2}{8}$) has two beats per measure; *triple meter* (e.g., $\frac{3}{4}$, $\frac{3}{2}$, $\frac{3}{8}$) has three beats per measure; *quadruple meter* (e.g., $\frac{4}{4}$, $\frac{4}{2}$, $\frac{4}{8}$) has four beats per measure.

	Time signatures	Beats per measure	Example
Duple meter:	$\frac{2}{4}$, $\frac{2}{2}$, $\frac{2}{8}$	2	
Triple meter:	$\frac{3}{4}$, $\frac{3}{2}$, $\frac{3}{8}$	3	
Quadruple meter:	$\frac{4}{4}$, $\frac{4}{2}$, $\frac{4}{8}$	4	

In most music, the first beat of each measure is stressed slightly, while the other beats are relatively unstressed.* This pattern is especially noticeable in marches and in dances. Composers create rhythmic interest or conflict by first establishing a pattern of stressed and unstressed beats as well as divisions of the beat, and then presenting music that disturbs this regularity. As a body of music literature, Scott Joplin's "rags" constitute an especially good illustration of this concept (see exercise 407), as do minuets and waltzes (see Strauss, *Blue Danube*

*Some theorists believe that in quadruple meter the third beat is also slightly stressed.

Waltz, page 157). In this first unit (Chapters 1–8) we will concentrate on rhythm patterns that generally adhere to the stressed/unstressed regularity of the beats within a given meter. In the chapters of Unit III we will introduce several rhythmic techniques that conflict with this sense of regularity.

Worksheet No. 3
Duple, Triple, and Quadruple Meters

Sing the songs below and identify the meter of each as duple, triple, or quadruple. The beat is indicated with an "**x**." If you feel the stress occurring every second beat, the meter is duple; if you feel the stress occurring every third beat, the meter is triple. Duple meter and quadruple meter may be indistinguishable at this point in your study.

1. "Deck the Halls" (in C major, start on G):
   Deck the halls with boughs of hol - ly,...
   x   x   x   x   x   x   x   x

2. "Take Me Out to the Ball Game" (in C major, start on C):
   Take me out to the ball game,...
   x x x   x   x   x   x x x x x x

3. "Jingle Bells" (in E♭ major, start on G), refrain:
   Jin - gle bells, jin - gle bells, jin - gle all the way,...
   x   x   x   x   x   x   x x

4. "Old MacDonald Had a Farm" (in G major, start on G):
   Old Mac - Don - ald had a farm, E - I - E - I - O!,...
   x   x   x   x   x x x   x x x x x x x x

5. "Baa, Baa, Black Sheep" (in C major, start on C):
   Baa, baa, black sheep, have you an - y wool,...
   x   x   x   x   x   x   x x

6. "Skip to My Lou" (in F major, start on A), refrain:
   Lou, Lou, skip to my Lou,...
   x   x   x   x

7. "Edelweiss" (in C major, start on E):
   E - del - weiss, E - del - weiss,...
   x x x   x x x x x x   x x x

8. "Rock-a-Bye Baby" (in G major, start on B):
   Rock - a - bye ba - by, on the tree top,...
   x x   x   x x x x x   x   x x x

One-part exercises

QUADRUPLE METER   We begin with exercises in quadruple meter, because the four-beat conducting pattern is easier to master than the two-beat or three-beat patterns. Practice the four-beat conducting pattern shown below. As you conduct, sing "Frère Jacques," silently or aloud, alone or as a class.

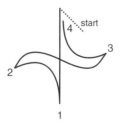

4 beats per measure
(e.g., $\frac{4}{4}$, $\frac{4}{2}$, $\frac{4}{8}$)

▸ Sing "Frère Jacques" (in F major, start on F):
Frè - re Jac - ques, Frè - re Jac - ques,
1   2   3   4   **1**   2   3   4

Dor - mez vous? Dor - mez vous?
1   2   3 4 **1**   2   3 4

Son - nez les ma - ti - nes, Son - nez les ma - ti - nes,
1   2   3   4 **1**   2   3   4

Din, dan, don, Din, dan, don.
1   2   3 4 **1**   2   3 4

Rhythm Cells

In the pages and chapters ahead, you will perform exercises composed of combinations and permutations of *rhythm cells.* Rhythm cells are individual notes or groups of notes that form the rhythmic building blocks of music. Each rhythmic cell is displayed in a box. A double bar marks the end of a cell. A bold "**x**" marks the location of the beat.

Unless otherwise directed by your instructor, perform the exercises below as follows:

- Sing "ta" on each note. Sing nothing on the rests.
- Conduct an empty measure immediately before you begin.
- Conduct while performing the entire exercise.

The first two rhythm cells, the *quarter note* and *quarter rest,* appear in the same box because they are so closely related.

This exercise is in quadruple meter.

Allegro

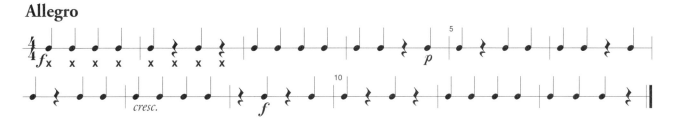

| HALF REST | The *half rest* ( ) always sits on top of a staff line. It usually appears on the middle line of a five-line staff ( ). |

| TIE | A *tie* (e.g.,) joins two notes of the same pitch, resulting in one uninterrupted sound that lasts the combined duration of the two notes. |

| NOTE ENDINGS | It is important that every note last the correct number of beats. A note *ends* exactly when the next note or rest *begins.* If a half note ( ) starts on the first beat of the measure, then it must end at the beginning of the third beat. (If this concept is confusing, try thinking of it in terms of a clock. Imagine that you have a two-hour class. If it starts at 1:00, then it will, of course, end at 3:00.) In the next exercise, the end of each sound of two-beat duration is marked with an arrow.

In this book, we will use horizontal brackets under notes (see below) to indicate rhythm patterns that sound the same but are notated differently. |

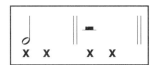

2

Preparatory drill

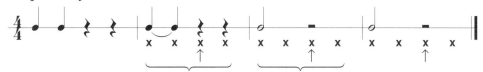

3

Allegro

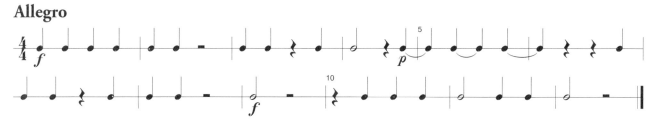

DUPLE METER   The next exercise is in duple meter. Practice conducting the two-beat pattern shown below, while singing "Yankee Doodle":

2 beats per measure
(e.g., $\frac{2}{4}, \frac{2}{2}, \frac{2}{8}$)

▸ Sing "Yankee Doodle" (in G major, start on G):

Yan - kee Doo - dle went to town a - rid - ing on a po - ny,
1　　　**2**　　**1**　　**2**　　**1**　　**2 1**　　**2**

Stuck a feath - er in his hat and called it mac - a - ro - ni.
1　　**2**　　**1**　　**2**　　　**1**　　**2**　　**1 2**

Yan - kee Doo - dle keep it up, Yan - kee Doo - dle dan - dy,
1　　　**2**　　**1**　**2 1**　　　**2**　　　**1 2**

Mind the mu - sic and the step, and with the girls be han - dy.
1　　　**2**　　**1**　　**2**　　**1**　　**2**　　**1 2**

4

Presto

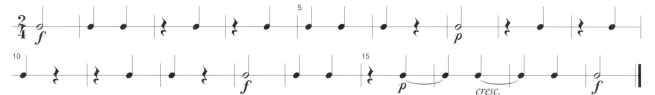

TRIPLE METER   The next exercises are in triple meter. Practice conducting the three-beat pattern below, while singing "America":

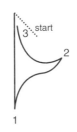

3 beats per measure
(e.g., $\frac{3}{4}$, $\frac{3}{2}$, $\frac{3}{8}$)

▸ Sing "America" (in C major, start on C):

My coun - try 'tis of thee,
1   2   3 1 2   3

Sweet land of lib - er - ty,
   1   2   3 1 2   3

Of thee I sing.
1   2   3 1   2   3

Land where my fa - thers died!
1   2   3 1 2   3

Land of the pil - grim's pride!
1   2   3 1   2   3

From ev - 'ry moun - tain - side,
1   2   3   1   2   3

Let free - dom ring!
1   2   3   1 2   3

AUGMENTATION DOT   A dot immediately following a note or rest is called an *augmentation dot*. This dot increases the length of the note or rest by one-half of its original value:

Dotted rests are rarely used in simple meter. They are, however, very common in compound meter, as we will see in Chapter 2.

5

Preparatory drill

6

Presto

In this exercise, be sure to hold each dotted half note (𝅗𝅥.) for three full beats, especially when it is followed by a rest.

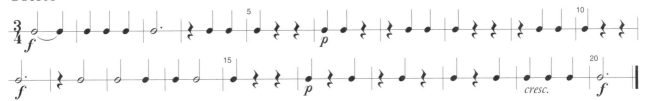

7

Allegro

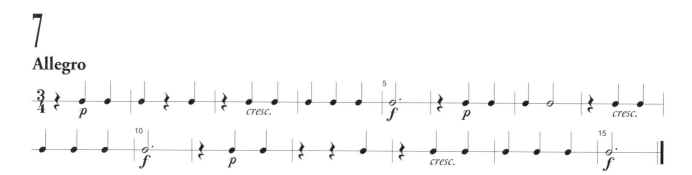

WHOLE NOTE AND
WHOLE-NOTE REST

The *whole-note rest* (ᴖ) always hangs below the line, usually below the second line of a five-line staff (ᴴ). (Compare this to the half rest, introduced on page 11.) Later in this chapter we will see that this symbol also signifies a whole-measure rest in any meter. In $\frac{4}{4}$, the *whole note* (o) ends on the first beat of the next measure.

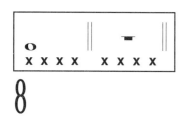

8

Preparatory drill

9

Presto

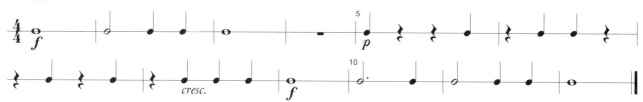

Worksheet No. 4
Note Endings

On what beat does each of the following notes end?

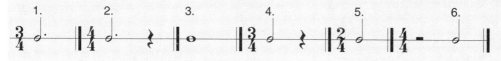

Speech Cues

Many of the cells introduced in *Rhythm Reading* fit in the space of one beat. You will learn these cells faster (and you will remember them longer) if, instead of singing "ta," you initially sing a word that closely resembles the cell in syllable lengths and accents. Such a word is called a *speech cue*. In this text many cells are introduced with a speech cue. It is likely that you are familiar with many of the rhythm cells that we introduce with speech cues. It is unlikely, however, that you are familiar with the many permutations in which the cells appear later in this book and in music literature. Speech cues may be the single most important tool in mastering the rhythmic component of music.

We suggest that you use a speech cue only for the preparatory drill that introduces a cell and for one full-length exercise, while continuing to sing "ta" on all other notes. This means that you will use only one speech cue in any given exercise. A complete list of the speech cues used in *Rhythm Reading* appears in Appendix C.

BEAMING   In the exercises below, beams are used to join eighth notes ( ) within the beat.

10

Preparatory drill   (recommended speech cue: "ba-ker")

11

Moderato

12

Allegretto

13

Allegro

To make this exercise more challenging, try adding a tie from the second eighth note of any eighth-note pair to the following note.

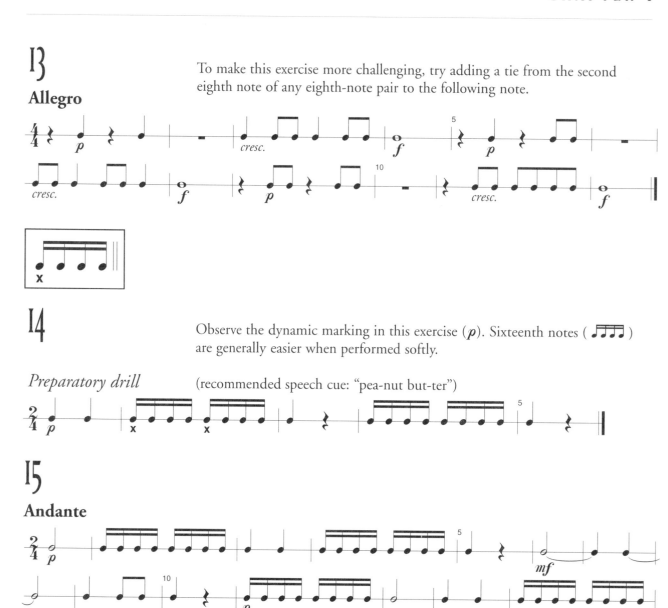

14

Observe the dynamic marking in this exercise (*p*). Sixteenth notes (♬) are generally easier when performed softly.

Preparatory drill   (recommended speech cue: "pea-nut but-ter")

15

Andante

COMMON TIME   The time signature ⁴⁄₄ is also indicated by the symbol **C**. Although **C** is often known as *common time,* it is not an abbreviation for this term. In the Middle Ages, the geometrically "perfect" circle stood for triple meter, the number three representing the "perfection" of the Holy Trinity. An "imperfect" half-circle stood for duple or quadruple meter. From this we use **C** to indicate ⁴⁄₄ .

16

Adagio

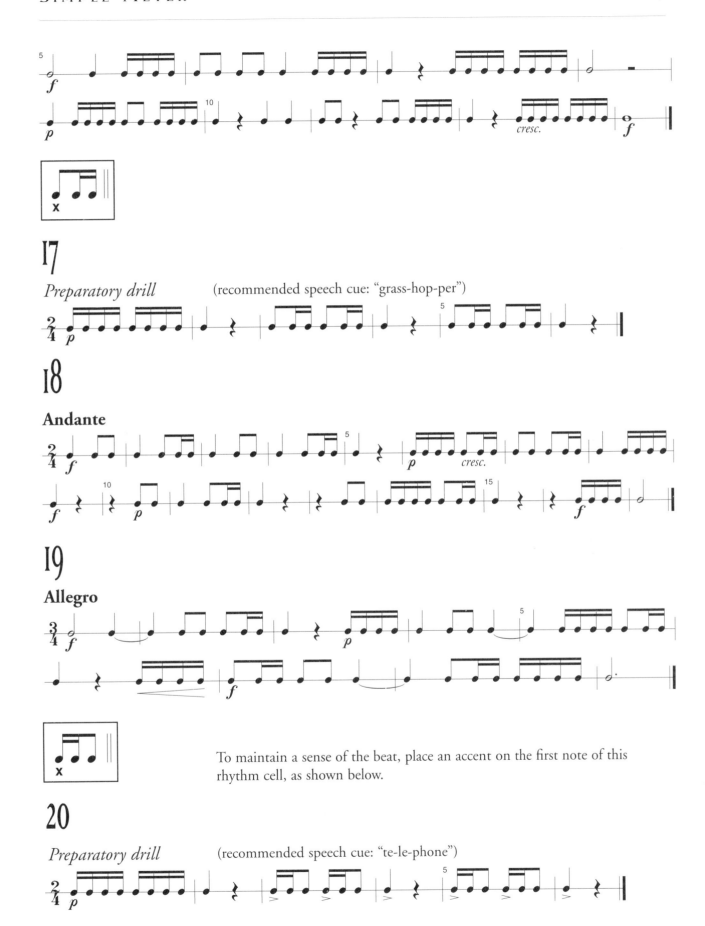

17

Preparatory drill   (recommended speech cue: "grass-hop-per")

18

Andante

19

Allegro

To maintain a sense of the beat, place an accent on the first note of this rhythm cell, as shown below.

20

Preparatory drill   (recommended speech cue: "te-le-phone")

21

Moderato

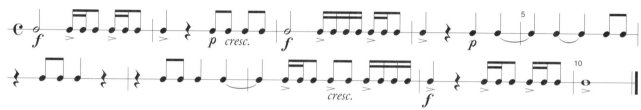

22

Allegro

In this exercise, be sure to choose a tempo that is slow enough to allow you to perform the measures with the fastest notes.

WHOLE-MEASURE
REST (−)

The symbol − has two meanings:

    1. Whole-note rest (− + − = −), e.g.,

$$\frac{4}{2} \quad o \quad - \quad | \quad \partial \quad \partial \quad - \quad \|$$

    2. *Whole-measure rest,* e.g.,

$$\frac{4}{2} \quad o \quad \partial \quad \partial \quad | \quad - \quad \| \frac{3}{4} \partial \quad \partial \quad | \quad - \quad \| \frac{3}{8} \partial \quad \flat \quad | \quad - \quad \|$$

If the rest stands alone in a measure, it indicates a whole-measure rest, regardless of the meter that is used. In the exercises below, take care to count the correct number of beats for each whole-measure rest.

METER CHANGES

When the meter changes within an exercise, you must also change your conducting pattern. In music literature, changes in meter can produce a striking effect, because stressed beats occur at irregular intervals.

23

Preparatory drill

24

Allegro

More challenging one-part exercises

COMPOSITE METERS

$\frac{5}{4}$ and $\frac{7}{4}$ are unusual examples of simple meter. Even though both have beats that are divided into two equal parts, each of their *measures* is divided into two or more unequal parts, thus producing an irregular accent pattern. These time signatures are examples of *composite meter*. In $\frac{5}{4}$, each measure can be divided into one part with 2 beats and one part with 3 beats, as $\frac{2}{4} + \frac{3}{4}$ or $\frac{3}{4} + \frac{2}{4}$. The division of the measure is often indicated with a dotted bar line, as shown below.

CONDUCTING IN $\frac{5}{4}$ (2 + 3)

Practice conducting the five-beat pattern for 2 + 3, given below. Note the grouping of beats: beats 1 and 2 are down or to the left and beats 3, 4, and 5 are up or to the right.

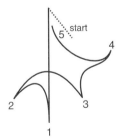

5 beats per measure (2 + 3)
(e.g., $\frac{5}{4}$, $\frac{5}{2}$, $\frac{5}{8}$)

25

Use the 2 + 3 conducting pattern for this exercise.

Andante (2 + 3)

CONDUCTING
IN 5/4 (3 + 2)

Now practice conducting the five-beat pattern for 3 + 2. Again, note the grouping of beats. In this case, beats 1, 2, and 3 are down or to the left and beats 4 and 5 are up or to the right.

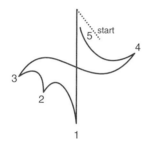

5 beats per measure (3 + 2)
(e.g., $\frac{5}{4}$, $\frac{5}{2}$, $\frac{5}{8}$)

26

Use the 3 + 2 conducting pattern.

Allegro (3 + 2)

CONDUCTING
IN 7/4

In the following 7/4 exercise, each measure is divided into a four-beat segment (as in 4/4) and a three-beat segment (as in 3/4). The actual seven-beat conducting pattern is rarely used. Instead, triple and quadruple patterns are generally combined, although sometimes duple plus triple plus duple is used. In the two exercises below, alternate between conducting in 4/4 and 3/4, or simply tap the beat.

27

Allegretto (4 + 3)

28

Allegro (3 + 4)

Two-part exercises for one person

These exercises are designed to improve your ability to follow two lines simultaneously. Perform both parts, using a combination of singing, tapping, or playing an instrument. Unless otherwise directed by your instructor, perform as follows:

- Tap each part with a different hand. Use two keys on a piano, or simply tap on a desk or table.

You may wish to add your own dynamics to these exercises.

29 — For Tuesday

Adagio

SING
TAP

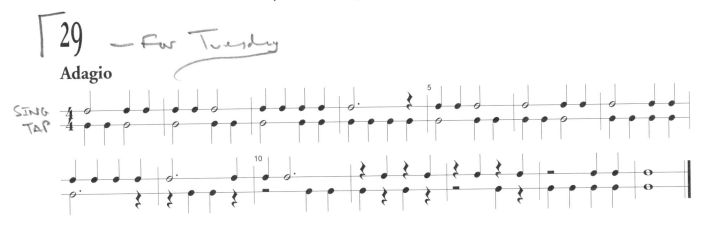

Andante

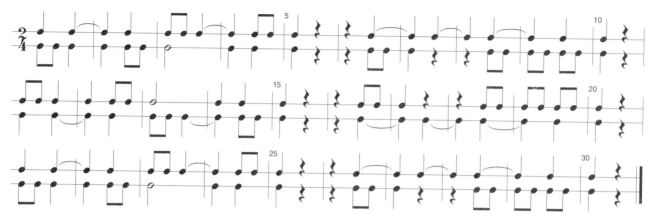

31

Adagio

Ensemble exercises

Perform these exercises with one or more persons to a part. Do not perform both parts yourself. To keep the lines of music distinct, sing the upper and lower parts on different pitches or on different syllables, such as "tee" and "too."

32

Allegro

CANON   In a *canon,* two or more voices (or instruments) perform identical melodies. Each voice enters at a specified time after the previous voice has begun. In the following canon, the second voice begins when the first voice reaches ②. Only the second voice will observe the fermata (⌢) in measure 19.

33

Allegro (Canon)

HOCKET   Exercise 34 (on the next page) is based on a rhythmic device known as *hocket.* The word "hocket" is related to a Latin word (*hoquetus*) meaning "hiccup." The term defies simple definition. The musical effect is that of a single melody split between two voices. The voices alternate rapidly, each singing only short fragments of the melody. Hocket frequently appears in music of the fourteenth century, such as in compositions of the French composer Guillaume de Machaut (ca.1300–1377). Examples of hocket appear below. Exercises 438 and 440 also feature hocket.

▸ Period of Petrus de Cruce, "Je cuidoie," top two voices, measures 17–18:

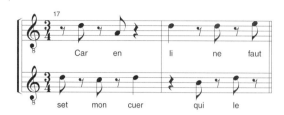

▸ Guillaume de Machaut, *Missa Notre Dame,* Gloria, top two voices, measures 120–125:*

34
Allegretto

Self-test on written concepts

1. How does simple meter differ from compound meter?

2. What is the beat unit in $\frac{3}{4}$? What is the beat unit in $\frac{2}{8}$?

3. How many beats are in a $\frac{4}{8}$ measure? How many beats are in a $\frac{2}{2}$ measure?

4. Give two examples of duple meter time signatures.

5. What are the two meanings for ▬ ?

---

*This passage is also frequently transcribed in $\frac{3}{2}$ meter.

6. Draw the conducting patterns for $\frac{2}{4}$, $\frac{3}{4}$, $\frac{4}{4}$, and $\frac{5}{4}$.

7. Write a half rest and a whole rest on a five-line staff.

8. "**C**" indicates what meter?

9. Give an example of composite meter. What is unusual about composite meter?

10. Circle the two rhythms below that sound the same.

11. Add an appropriate time signature for each of the following measures. Use the boxes provided.

12. Each measure below is incomplete. How many beats are missing from each measure?

13. Indicate the location of each beat with an "**x**" (or a vertical line). The quarter note is the beat unit. The first measure is already done.

14. Write and perform two rhythm exercises incorporating the rhythm notation introduced in this chapter. Beams should join notes within the beat.

a. Write and perform an exercise using each of the following at least once:

b. Write and perform an exercise using each of the following at least once:

Recommended listening

SIMPLE METER

- Johann Sebastian Bach, Brandenburg Concerto No. 2 in F Major, BWV 1047: third movement (Allegro assai)

- Johannes Brahms, Symphony No. 4 in E Minor, Op. 98: third movement (Allegro giocoso)

- Franz Joseph Haydn, Concerto in E♭ Major for Trumpet and Orchestra: first movement (Allegro) and third movement (Rondo: Allegro)

- Franz Joseph Haydn, Symphony No. 94 in G Major ("Surprise"): third movement (Andante)

- Wolfgang Amadeus Mozart, Symphony No. 40 in G Minor, K. 550: first movement (Allegro molto)

- John Philip Sousa, *The Stars and Stripes Forever*

COMPOUND METER

- Johann Sebastian Bach, Brandenburg Concerto No. 6 in B♭ Major, BWV 1051: third movement (Allegro)

- Johann Sebastian Bach, Partita No. 3 in A Minor, BWV 827: Gigue

- Johann Sebastian Bach, Suite for Solo Cello No. 4 in E♭ Major, BWV 1010: Gigue

- Johann Sebastian Bach, Suite for Solo Cello No. 6 in D Major, BWV 1012: Prelude and Gigue

- Archangelo Corelli, Sonata for Violin in D Minor, Op. 5, No. 7: fourth movement (Giga)

- Archangelo Corelli, Sonata for Violin in E Minor, Op. 5, No. 8: fourth movement (Giga)

- Gabriel Fauré, Sicilienne (from *Pelléas et Mélisande*)

- Wolfgang Amadeus Mozart, Clarinet Concerto in A Major, K. 622: third movement (Rondo: Allegro)

- Wolfgang Amadeus Mozart, Piano Concerto in B♭ Major, K. 595: third movement (Allegro)

QUADRUPLE METER

- Johannes Brahms, Symphony No. 3 in F Major: second movement (Allegro moderato)

- Johann Pachelbel, Canon in D Major

- Wolfgang Amadeus Mozart, Concerto in C Major for Piano and Orchestra, K. 467: first movement (Allegro maestoso)

DUPLE METER

- Johann Sebastian Bach, *The Art of Fugue,* BWV 1080: Contrapunctus 1 (theme)

- Franz Joseph Haydn, Symphony No. 104 in D Major ("London"): fourth movement (Finale: Spiritoso)

TRIPLE METER

- Georges Bizet, *Carmen Suite:* Danse bohème (Chanson bohème, Act II)

- Johannes Brahms, Symphony No. 2 in D Major, Op. 73: first movement (Allegro non troppo)

- Franz Joseph Haydn, Symphony No. 45 in F♯ Minor ("Farewell"): first movement (Allegro assai)

- Wolfgang Amadeus Mozart, Concerto No. 1 in G Major, K. 313: third movement (Rondo: Tempo di Minuetto)

- Antonio Vivaldi, *The Four Seasons,* "Autumn": third movement (Allegro)

COMPOSITE METER (2 + 3)

- Pytr Il'yich Tchaikovsky, Symphony No. 6 in B Minor ("Pathétique"): second movement (Allegro con grazia)

- Alexander Borodin, Symphony No. 3 in A Minor (unfinished): second movement (Scherzo: Vivo)

- Maurice Ravel, String Quartet in F Major: fourth movement (Vif et agité)

COMPOSITE METER (3 + 2)

- Gustav Holst, *The Planets,* Op. 32: seventh movement ("Neptune, the Mystic")

2

Compound meter

Time signatures for compound meters

The exercises in this chapter are in *compound meter.* To review the difference
between simple and compound meters, reread the first section of Chapter 1
("Simple and Compound Meters") and sing the two songs discussed in that
section.

Generally speaking, if the top number of a time signature is 6, 9, or 12 (or
another multiple of three) the meter is compound. In compound meter, the
beat is usually divided into *three* equal parts (not *two,* as in simple meter). The
bottom number of the time signature indicates the rhythmic value not of the
beat (as in simple meter), but of the *division of the beat.* This rhythmic value is
known as the *division unit.* The upper number of a compound-meter time
signature indicates the number of divisions in each measure. In $\frac{6}{8}$, for example,
the division unit is the eighth note, and each measure contains six divisions:

Compound Meter

6 → six divisions in each measure
8 → the eighth note is the division unit

Worksheet No. 5
Compound-Meter Time Signatures: The Division Unit

For each of the compound meter time signatures listed below, determine the rhythmic value of the division unit and the number of divisions per measure.

1. $\frac{6}{4}$ 2. $\frac{12}{8}$ 3. $\frac{9}{4}$ 4. $\frac{15}{16}$ 5. $\frac{9}{16}$ 6. $\frac{12}{4}$ 7. $\frac{9}{8}$ 8. $\frac{12}{16}$

Worksheet No. 6
Compound Meter vs. Simple Meter

Identify each time signature below as simple or compound meter.

1. $\frac{9}{4}$ 2. $\frac{2}{4}$ 3. $\frac{12}{8}$ 4. $\frac{4}{16}$ 5. $\frac{4}{8}$ 6. $\frac{12}{4}$ 7. $\frac{6}{4}$ 8. $\frac{21}{16}$

In compound meter, each group of three divisions receives one beat. In $\frac{6}{8}$, for example, each group of three eighth notes receives one beat. Sing the line of rhythm below. Use the speech cue *Bee-tho-ven* for each group of three eighth notes; tap the beats shown.

Each beat has the rhythmic value of a dotted quarter note (𝅘𝅥𝅮𝅘𝅥𝅮𝅘𝅥𝅮 = 𝅘𝅥.). Therefore, we usually count $\frac{6}{8}$ in two rather than in six. Sing the following:

Another compound meter is $\frac{12}{4}$. In $\frac{12}{4}$, each measure contains twelve quarter-note divisions. Each group of three quarter notes receives one beat:

The rhythmic value of each beat is a dotted half note (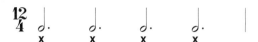):

$$\mathbf{\frac{12}{4}} \quad \overset{}{\underset{x}{\mathbf{\textit{d.}}}} \quad \overset{}{\underset{x}{\mathbf{\textit{d.}}}} \quad \overset{}{\underset{x}{\mathbf{\textit{d.}}}} \quad \overset{}{\underset{x}{\mathbf{\textit{d.}}}} \quad \Big|$$

To figure out the number of beats per measure in compound meter, divide the top number of the time signature by three. To figure out the rhythmic value of the beat, triple the note value indicated by the lower number of the time signature:

6 → six divisions in each measure   →   6 ÷ 3 = 2   →   2 beats per measure
8 → the eighth note is the division unit → ♪ + ♪ + ♪ = ♩. → ♩. is the beat unit

Note that the beat unit in compound meter is always a dotted note. This explains why time signatures for compound meter refer to the division unit rather than the beat unit. If | ♩ ♩ | = ²⁄₄ (simple meter), then how could we write a time signature for | ♩. ♩. | (compound meter) that specifies two beats to the measure? In fact, it could be written as ²₍.₎; but this notation is rarely used except in music of the twentieth century.

Worksheet No. 7
Compound Meter Time Signatures: The Beat Unit

For each of the compound meters listed below, determine the number of beats per measure and the beat unit.

1. ⁶⁄₄   2. ¹²⁄₈   3. ⁹⁄₄   4. ¹⁵⁄₁₆   5. ⁹⁄₁₆   6. ¹²⁄₄   7. ⁹⁄₈   8. ¹²⁄₁₆

Examples of compound meter appear below. Note that in compound meter the top number of the time signature is always divisible by three.

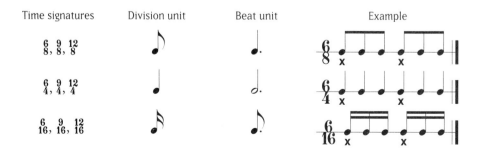

Time signatures	Division unit	Beat unit	Example
⁶⁄₈, ⁹⁄₈, ¹²⁄₈	♪	♩.	
⁶⁄₄, ⁹⁄₄, ¹²⁄₄	♩	♩.	
⁶⁄₁₆, ⁹⁄₁₆, ¹²⁄₁₆	♬	♪.	

Compound duple, triple, and quadruple meters with a dotted quarter-note beat

Compound meters (just like simple meters) are categorized as duple, triple, or quadruple, according to the number of beats per measure. *In all exercises in compound meter, be sure to count the appropriate number of beats per measure:*

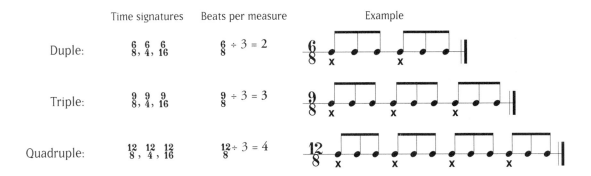

	Time signatures	Beats per measure	Example
Duple:	$\frac{6}{8}, \frac{6}{4}, \frac{6}{16}$	$\frac{6}{8} \div 3 = 2$	
Triple:	$\frac{9}{8}, \frac{9}{4}, \frac{9}{16}$	$\frac{9}{8} \div 3 = 3$	
Quadruple:	$\frac{12}{8}, \frac{12}{4}, \frac{12}{16}$	$\frac{12}{8} \div 3 = 4$	

One-part exercises

Conduct using the conducting patterns you used for simple meter. In $\frac{6}{8}$, conduct two beats per measure (as in $\frac{2}{4}$).

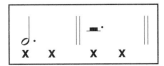

35
Preparatory drill

36

In $\frac{12}{8}$, conduct four beats per measure (as in $\frac{4}{4}$).

Preparatory drill

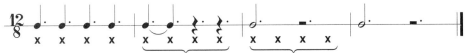

37
Allegro

38

In $\frac{9}{8}$, conduct three beats per measure (as in $\frac{3}{4}$).

Presto

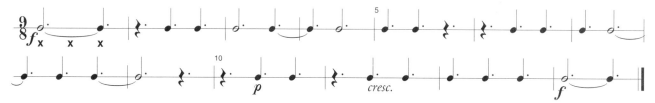

39

Preparatory drill

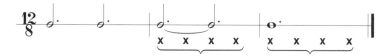

Speech Cues

Remember to use a speech cue only for the preparatory drill that introduces a cell and for one full-length exercise. Then return to singing "ta" for all notes. This means that you will use only one speech cue in any given exercise.

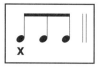

40

Preparatory drill   (recommended speech cue: "Bee-tho-ven")

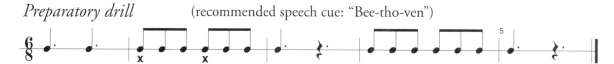

41

Andante

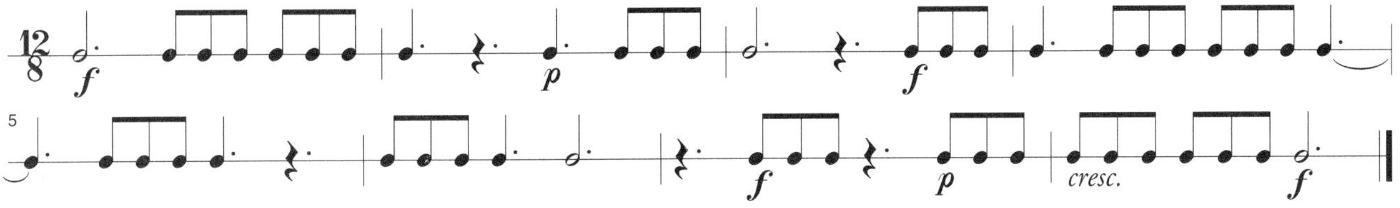

42

Preparatory drill   (recommended speech cue: "ti-kee ti-kee ti-kee"*)

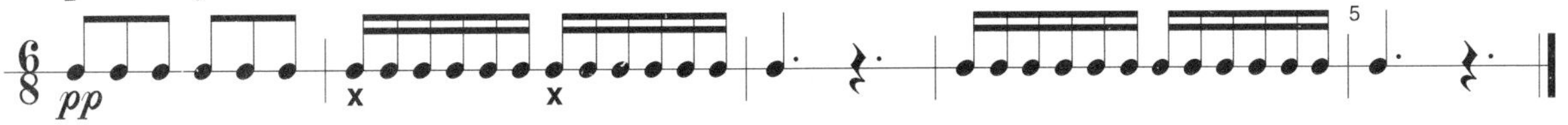

43

Andante

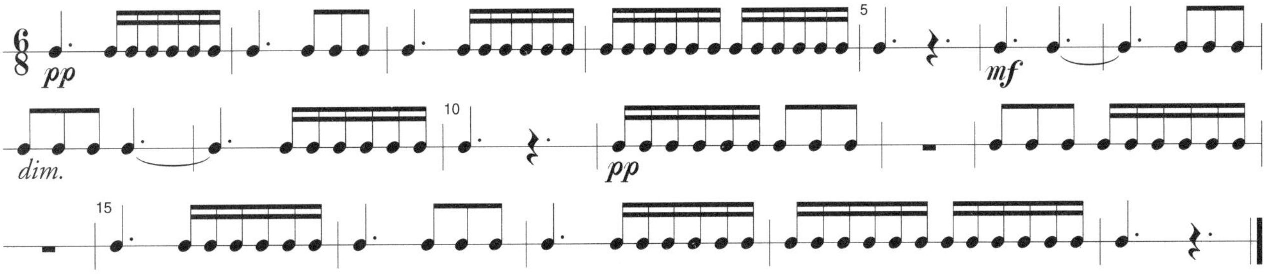

44

Preparatory drill   (recommended speech cue: "ta ti-kee ti-kee")

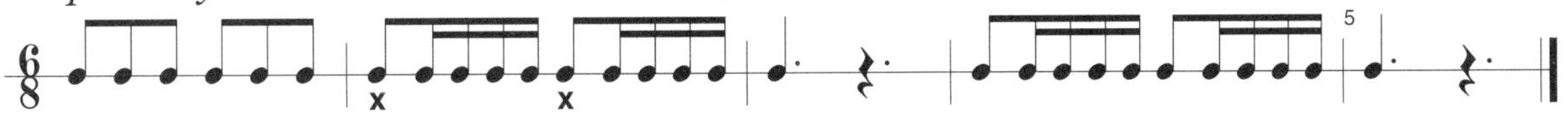

---

*For pronunciation, note that "ti-kee" rhymes with "sticky."

45

To help maintain the beat, add accents as shown in this exercise.

Preparatory drill   (recommended speech cue: "ti-kee ti-kee ta")

46

Andante

50

Adagio

In this exercise, be sure to change your conducting pattern when the time signature changes.

51

Moderato

52

In this preparatory drill, accents are included to ensure proper placement of the beat.

Preparatory drill   (recommended speech cue: "ti-kee ta ti-kee")

53
Adagio

More challenging one-part exercises

54
Presto

In this exercise, the first beat of nearly every measure is obscured by a tie across the barline. Perform as quickly as possible.

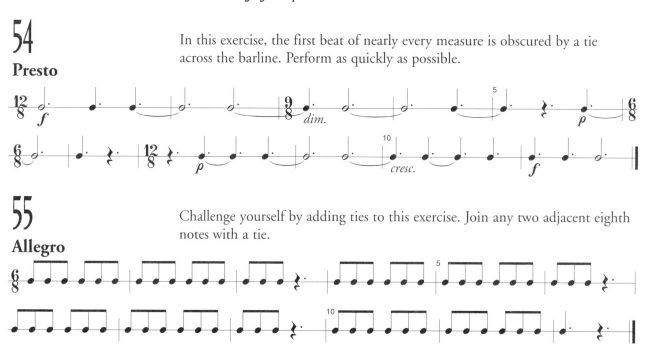

55
Allegro

Challenge yourself by adding ties to this exercise. Join any two adjacent eighth notes with a tie.

ONE BEAT PER MEASURE   In music in $\frac{3}{8}$, $\frac{3}{4}$, and $\frac{3}{16}$ at a fast tempo, it is common to count each measure as one beat rather than counting three beats per measure. Practice the one-beat conducting pattern shown below, while singing "We Three Kings."

1 beat per measure
(e.g., $\frac{3}{8}$, $\frac{3}{4}$, $\frac{3}{16}$ at a fast tempo)

▶ Sing "We Three Kings" (in C minor, start on G):

We three kings of O - ri - ent are,
1   1   1   1

Bear - ing gifts we trav - erse a - far,
1   1   1   1

Field and foun - tain, moor and moun - tain, fol - low - ing yon - der star.
1   1   1   1   1   1   1

Professional performers generally count one beat per measure when playing fast passages in $\frac{3}{8}$, $\frac{3}{4}$, and $\frac{3}{16}$. Whether or not these meters are actually compound is a debatable point. Some music theorists claim that these meters are never compound regardless of the tempo of the passage. Others feel that a fast waltz or scherzo notated in $\frac{3}{4}$ is in compound meter, one beat per measure.* For example, Beethoven marks the opening of his third symphony (in $\frac{3}{4}$) as ♩. = 60, thereby suggesting compound meter. (See exercise 400.)

56

Count one beat per measure.

Allegretto

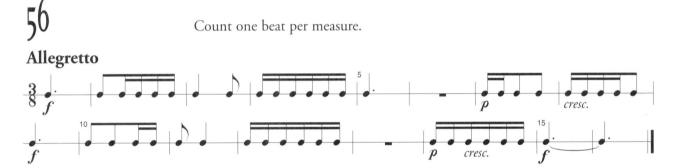

BEAMING OVER RESTS

Exercise 57 introduces a type of rhythmic notation frequently found in music of the twentieth century: beaming over rests. This type of beaming helps the performer visually group notes into beats where rests tend to obscure the beat. (For examples of this type of notation in music literature, see exercises 416, 429, 442, and 466.)

Exercise 57 is based on cells introduced earlier in this chapter, with some notes of each cell replaced with rests. The following illustration shows how individual measures in this exercise are derived from rhythm cells that you have already learned:

rhythm pattern:

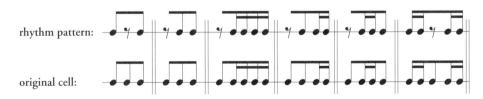

original cell:

*See Stephen Kostka and Dorothy Payne, *Tonal Harmony: With an Introduction to Twentieth-Century Music,* 3rd ed. (New York: McGraw-Hill, 1995), p. 36.

This style of notation will be used frequently throughout *Rhythm Reading,* to help remind you of the original cell on which each rhythm pattern is based.

57

Allegretto

In this exercise, practice especially difficult measures by first practicing with notes in place of the rests. Count one beat per measure.

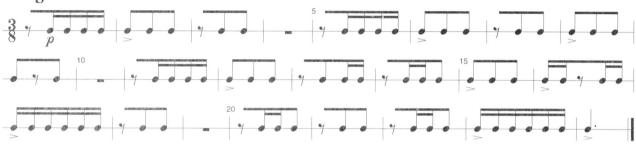

Two-part exercises for one person

THE ✕ SIGN   The symbol ✕ indicates that the performer should repeat the previous measure.

58

Adagio

59

Allegro (Canon)

Count one beat per measure.

Ensemble exercise for more than one person

RETROGRADE CANON   The following duet is a *retrograde canon*, also known as a crab canon or canon cancrizans. ("Cancrizans" is Latin for "crab-like.") The lower part is the retrograde (backward) version of the top part.

60

Allegretto (Retrograde Canon)

Review exercise

61

This exercise reviews cells and meters introduced in Chapter 1.

Allegro

Self-test on written concepts

1. How does compound meter differ from simple meter?

2. Differentiate between the terms "beat unit" and "division unit."

3. In $\frac{9}{8}$,

    a. What does the "9" mean?

    b. What does the "8" mean?

    c. What is the beat unit?

4. What does the symbol ⁒ mean?

5. Circle the two rhythms below that sound identical.

6. The following line of music is beamed incorrectly. Renotate the entire line, using beams to join notes within the beat.

7. Indicate the location of each beat with an "**x**" (or a vertical line). The dotted quarter note is the beat unit. The first measure is already done.

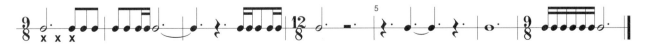

8. Write and perform two rhythm exercises incorporating the rhythmic notation introduced in this chapter. Beams should join notes within the beat.

a. Write and perform an exercise using each of the following at least once:

b. Write and perform an exercise using each of the following at least once:

Recommended listening

See the end of Chapter 1 (page 26) for recommended listening, including excerpts in simple and compound meters.

3

Simple meter: Quarter-note beat

This chapter builds on fundamental rhythm patterns in simple meter with a quarter-note beat, first introduced in Chapter 1.

One-part exercises

62

Preparatory drill

63

Moderato

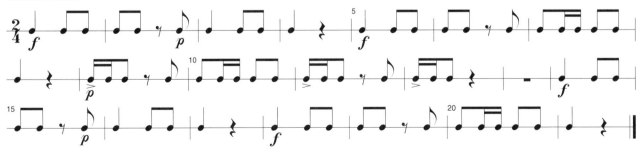

64

Andante

65

Preparatory drill

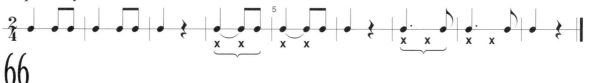

66

Allegro

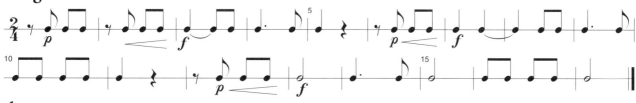

67

Allegretto

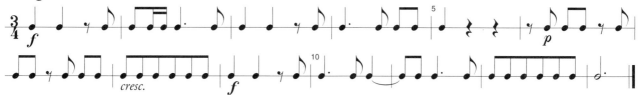

68

Andante

ANACRUSIS

Exercise 69 begins with an *anacrusis,* also known as an upbeat or a pickup. An anacrusis is one or more notes that appear before the first complete measure of a composition or movement. The last measure lacks the same number of beats as appear in the anacrusis. Measure numbering begins with the first complete measure.

Many well-known songs begin with an anacrusis. Try some examples by singing the songs below. In each case the anacrusis is indicated with bold text.

Songs with anacrusis

- Sing "The Star-Spangled Banner" (in A♭ major, start on E♭):

  Oh, say can you see, by the dawn's early light,...

- Sing "We Wish You a Merry Christmas" (in G major, start on D):

  We wish you a merry Christmas,...

- Sing "O Come All Ye Faithful" (in A♭ major, start on A♭):

  O come all ye faithful, Joyful and triumphant,...

In contrast, the following songs do not begin with an anacrusis:

Songs without anacrusis

- Sing "Row, Row, Row Your Boat" (in C major, start on C):

  Row, row, row your boat...

- Sing "Deck the Halls" (in C major, start on G):

  Deck the halls with boughs of holly,...

- Sing "Jack and Jill" (in G major, start on G):

  Jack and Jill went up the hill, To fetch a pail of water;...

Worksheet No. 8
Anacrusis

Sing the songs listed below. Identify each song as having or not having an anacrusis.

1. "America" (in C major, start on C)
2. "Frère Jacques" (in C major, start on C)
3. "Joy to the World" (in D major, start on D)
4. "Away in a Manger" (in F major, start on C)

5. "The First Noel" (in D major, start on F♯)
6. "Jingle Bells," refrain (in E♭ major, start on G)
7. "The Farmer in the Dell" (in D major, start on A)
8. "Skip to My Lou" (in F major, start on A)

Conduct an empty partial measure as you begin an exercise with an anacrusis. For example, in the following exercise, you will conduct beats 1 and 2 before singing on beat 3.

Allegretto

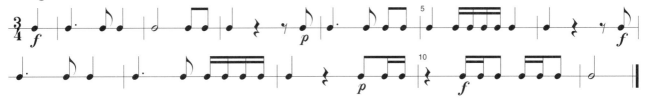

Allegro

MULTI-MEASURE RESTS

A rest of more than one measure is notated with a heavy horizontal bar and a numeral indicating the number of measures of silence. For example, a seven-measure rest is notated as follows:

Many publishers, however, reserve the above notation for rests of nine or more measures. For rests of shorter duration, the following three symbols are used alone or in combination:

Symbol	Duration
	1 measure
	2 measures
	4 measures

A three-measure rest, then, may be notated as follows:

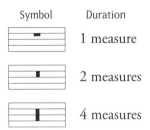

71

Andante

72

Preparatory drill (recommended speech cue: "to-day")

73

Adagio

74

Andante

75

Preparatory drill   (recommended speech cue: "pas-ta"*)

76

Andante

*Elongate and accent the first syllable of "pas-ta."

Andante

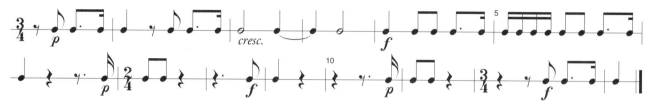

INVERTED DOTTING

The rhythm is an example of *inverted dotting*. It is the mirror image of the more familiar pattern, introduced above. Inverted dotting is also commonly known as a Scotch snap because it appears frequently in Scottish folk tunes, for example:

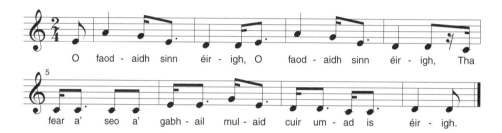

O faod - aidh sinn éir - igh, O faod - aidh sinn éir - igh, Tha

fear a' seo a' gabh - ail mul - aid cuir um - ad is éir - igh.

This rhythm also occurs frequently in Hungarian music, for example:

Há - la Is - ten, makk is van, Majd mëg - hí - zik a kis kan.

Ha mëg - hí - zik, lë - vág - juk, Majd ta - risz - nyá - ba rak - juk.

To maintain a sense of the beat, place an accent on the first note of this rhythm cell, as shown below. When a rhythm cell is presented in a bracketed version (as below), use the suggested speech cue for both versions of the cell.

Preparatory drill   (recommended speech cue: "ta-ble")

79

Allegro

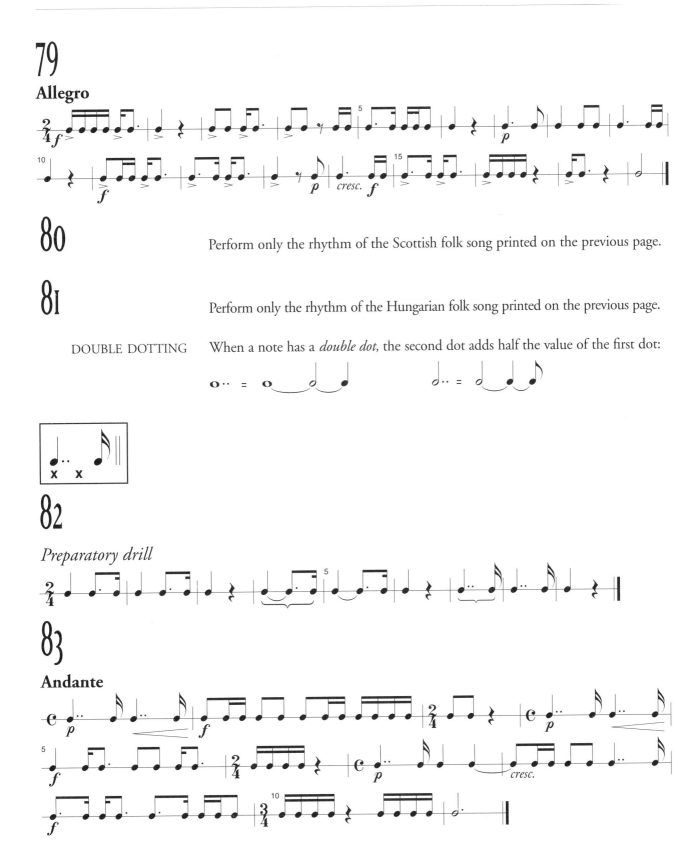

80   Perform only the rhythm of the Scottish folk song printed on the previous page.

81   Perform only the rhythm of the Hungarian folk song printed on the previous page.

DOUBLE DOTTING   When a note has a *double dot,* the second dot adds half the value of the first dot:

82

Preparatory drill

83

Andante

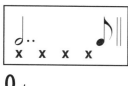

84

Preparatory drill

85

Allegro

86

Allegro

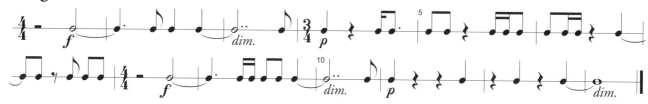

MEASURED TREMOLO

Measured tremolo is a notational shorthand used most often in orchestral music and piano reductions of orchestral music. A series of repeated notes (e.g., 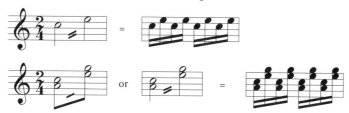) is indicated by a note with one or more slashes (e.g.,). The *speed* of the tremolo is indicated by the total number of slashes plus the total number of beams or flags. The *duration* of the tremolo is indicated by the rhythmic value of the note itself (i.e., without the slash or slashes):

A tremolo between two different notes or chords is also used. Note that in this type of tremolo the note value is given twice:

This type of tremolo is less common than the first type; it will not appear in any exercises in this text.

Worksheet No. 9
Measured Tremolo

Rewrite the following measured tremolos using non-tremolo notation.

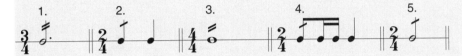

Rewrite the following rhythms using tremolo notation wherever possible.

Music can also have unmeasured tremolos. They are usually notated with three or four slashes, as shown below in the second movement of Claude Debussy's *La mer* (opening measures). With unmeasured tremolos, the note or notes are repeated as quickly as possible.

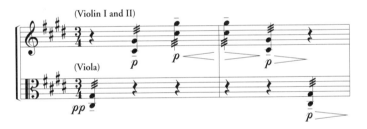

All tremolos that appear in *Rhythm Reading* are measured; in other words, you must perform the actual rhythmic values indicated by the tremolo notation.

This exercise is written twice, once with tremolo notation and once without.

Moderato

88

Moderato

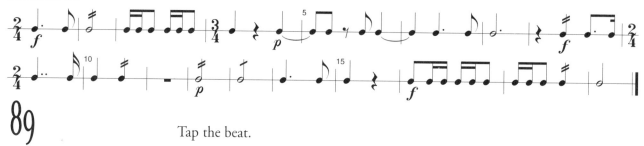

89

Tap the beat.

Allegretto

More challenging one-part exercises

90

Tap the beat.

Andante

91

Adagio

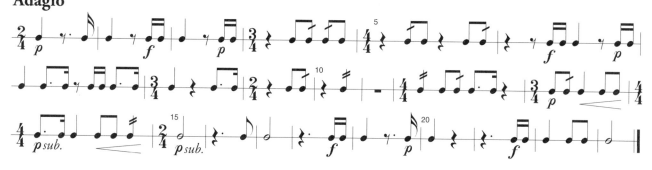

92

Tap the beat.

Allegro

Two-part exercises for one person

93

Adagio

94

Andante

Ensemble exercises

95

This canon uses hocket. To review this concept, turn to Chapter 1, pages 23–24.

Allegro (Retrograde Canon)

AUGMENTATION CANON

The following exercise is an *augmentation canon*. The lower part is the same as the upper part except that all the note values are doubled. For example, where the upper part has a quarter note, the lower part has a half note. Note the relationship between the two voices in measure 1:

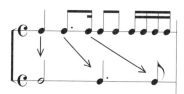

96

Compare this exercise to exercise 152, which is a diminution canon.

Presto (Augmentation Canon)

97

In this exercise, the effect is hocket (see Chapter 1, pages 23–24).

Allegro

Self-test on written concepts

1. What is an anacrusis?

2. Circle the anacrusis in the following example:

3. What is wrong with the following example?

4. Rewrite the following measured tremolos using non-tremolo notation:

a. ♩. =   b. 𝆯 =   c. ♩ =

5. Circle the *two* pairs of identical rhythms below.

6. Add an appropriate time signature to the following line of music:

7. Indicate the location of each beat with an "**x**" (or a vertical line). The quarter note is the beat unit.

8. Write and perform two rhythm exercises incorporating the rhythmic notation introduced in this chapter.

a. Write and perform an exercise using each of the following at least once:

and tremolo

b. Write and perform an exercise using each of the following at least once:

and anacrusis

Compound meter: Dotted quarter-note beat

This chapter builds on fundamental rhythm patterns in compound meters that have a dotted quarter-note beat, first introduced in Chapter 2.

One-part exercises

98

Preparatory drill   (recommended speech cue: "la-zy")

99

Allegretto

ONE BEAT PER MEASURE   For the next exercise, conduct 1 beat per measure. Use the following
conducting pattern:

1 beat per measure
(e.g., $\frac{3}{8}$, $\frac{3}{4}$, $\frac{3}{16}$ at a fast tempo)

100

Allegro

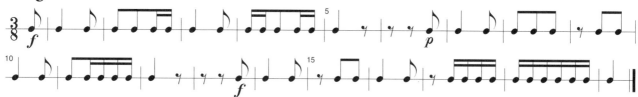

101

Preparatory drill   (recommended speech cue: "la-zi-ly")

102

Beams over rests should help you group the notes into beats.

Moderato

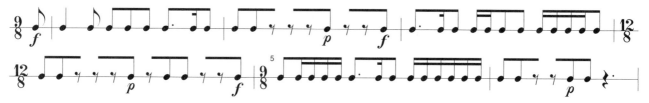

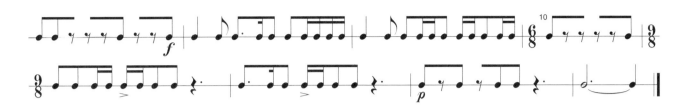

103

Preparatory drill (recommended speech cue: "la-zi-lee-kee")

104

Allegro

To ensure accurate performance of this cell, place accents as shown below. Remember to use the suggested speech cue for both versions of the cell in the preparatory drill.

105

Preparatory drill (recommended speech cue: "jum-bo")

106

Allegro

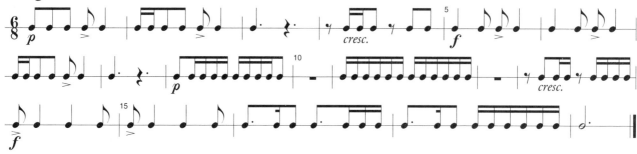

107

Moderato

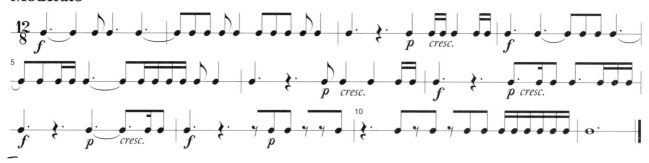

108

The accents shown in this exercise will help produce accuracy and adherence to the beat.

Preparatory drill   (recommended speech cue: "some-bo-dy")

109

Andante

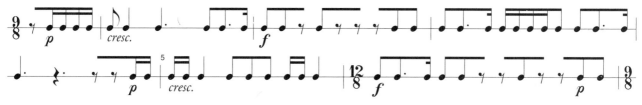

110

Preparatory drill　　　　(recommended speech cue: "bu-sy-bo-dy")

111

Allegretto

112

Preparatory drill

113

Allegretto

114

Preparatory drill

115

Allegretto

MEASURED TREMOLO   The rules for interpreting measured tremolo are the same for compound meter as they are for simple meter: The *speed* of the tremolo is indicated by the total number of slashes plus the total number of beams or flags. The *duration* of the tremolo is indicated by the rhythmic value of the note itself (i.e., without the slash or slashes). For example:

For further information on measured tremolo, see page 50.

116

This exercise is written twice, once with tremolo notation and once without.

Allegro

117

Allegro

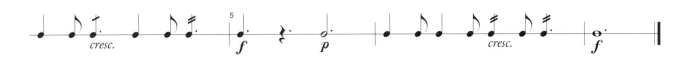

More challenging one-part exercises

FINAL

118

In this exercise, add your own dynamics. Count one beat per measure.

Allegro

119

Presto

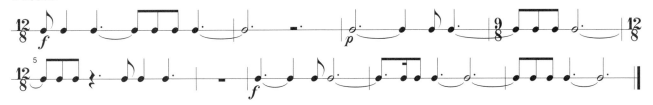

SPLIT MEASURES   In meters such as $\frac{12}{8}$ and $\frac{12}{4}$, printed measures tend to be unusually long. As a result, such measures may be split across lines of music, much as words are split across lines in written language. Note that there is no bar line at the end of the first line of the following exercise.

120

Adagio

Two-part exercises for one person

121

Adagio

122

Andante

Ensemble exercise

123

Allegro (Theme and Variations)

Review exercise

124

Andante

This exercise reviews the cells and meters introduced in Chapters 1 and 3. Tap the beat.

Self-test on written concepts

1. Indicate the location of each beat with an "**x**" (or a vertical line). The dotted quarter note is the beat unit.

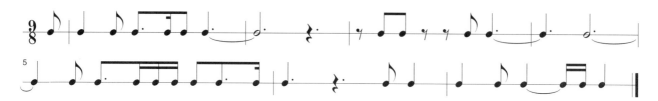

2. Rewrite the following rhythms using tremolo notation:

3. The following line of music is beamed incorrectly. Renotate the entire line, using beams to join notes within the beat whenever possible.

4. Write and perform two rhythm exercises incorporating the rhythmic notation introduced in this chapter.

   a. Write and perform an exercise using each of the following at least once:

 and measured tremolo

   b. Write and perform an exercise using each of the following at least once:

SIMPLE METER: HALF-NOTE BEAT

Equivalent cells

The following two measures are equivalent:

Because of the meters used, each note receives one beat. The difference between the two meters is the beat unit: In $\frac{2}{4}$, the *quarter note* receives one beat; in $\frac{2}{2}$, the *half note* receives one beat. The following measures are also equivalent, because each note receives two beats.

In this and the following three chapters, previously learned rhythm cells will be reintroduced as equivalent patterns in meters with different beat units.

The present chapter, based on the half-note beat, reintroduces cells first presented in Chapters 1 and 3 with a quarter-note beat.

Worksheet No. 10
Equivalent Cells: Simple Meter, $\frac{x}{4} \rightarrow \frac{x}{2}$

Rewrite each of the following lines of rhythm using a half-note beat. In your new version, indicate the location of each beat with an "**x**" (or a vertical line). As a model, the first example has already been rewritten. This material is not intended to be performed.

One-part exercises

125

Preparatory drill

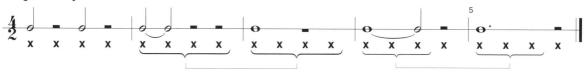

---

*For a discussion of the double whole note (𝄎) and the double whole rest (▪), see p. 69.

126

Allegretto

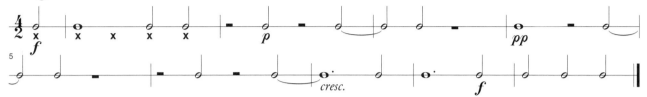

127

Allegretto

DOUBLE WHOLE NOTE;   The double whole note, also known as a *breve*, may be notated as ▯𝗈▯ or ◫ .
DOUBLE WHOLE REST   The double whole rest appears on a five-line staff as follows: ▭▪ .

128

In $\frac{4}{2}$ meter, the double whole note and double whole rest each receives four beats.

Presto

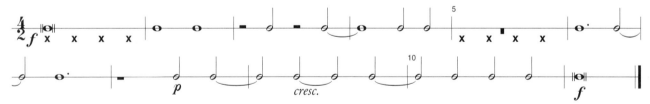

Speech Cues for Cells with a Half-Note Beat

Suggested speech cues for cells with a half-note beat (e.g., $\frac{2}{2}$, $\frac{3}{2}$, and $\frac{4}{2}$) are the same as for the equivalent cells with a quarter-note beat (e.g., $\frac{2}{4}$, $\frac{3}{4}$, and $\frac{4}{4}$). For example, in preparatory drill 129 you should again use the speech cues "baker" and "peanut butter." Appendix C lists all of the speech cues introduced in *Rhythm Reading* in terms of a quarter-note beat or a dotted quarter-note beat.

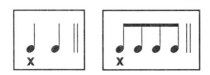

129

Preparatory drill

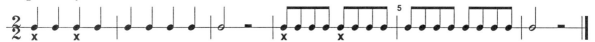

ALLA BREVE   The time signature ⅖ is also known as *alla breve* or *cut time*, and may be notated as ₵ (₵ "cut in half").

130

Moderato

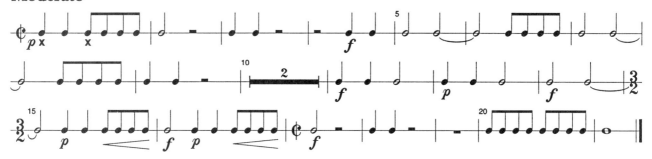

131

Preparatory drill

132

Moderato

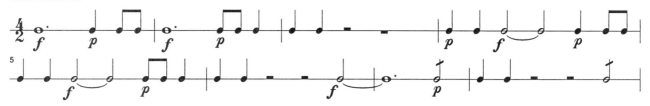

133

Moderato

This exercise uses composite meter (see pages 19–21). The dotted bar lines divide each measure into two unequal halves. Tap the beat.

134

Preparatory drill

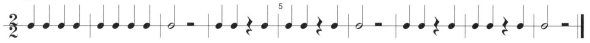

135

Allegro

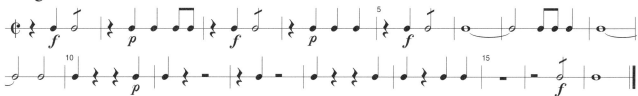

136

Preparatory drill

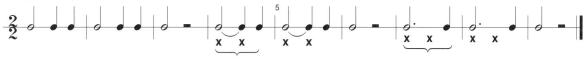

137

Allegro

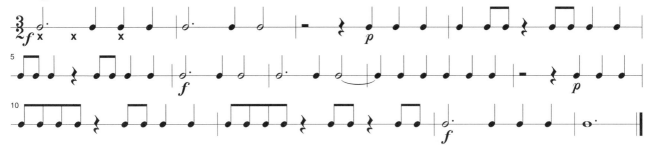

138

Preparatory drill

139

Preparatory drill

140

Allegro

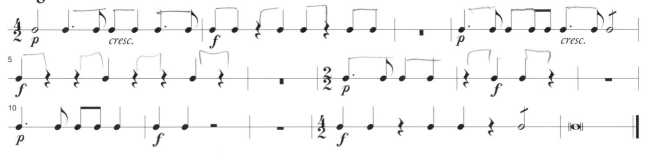

141

Preparatory drill

142

Allegretto

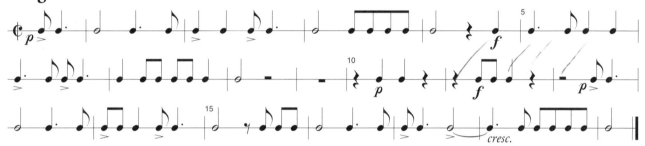

143

Preparatory drill

144

Moderato

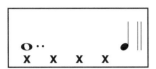

145

Preparatory drill

146

Allegro

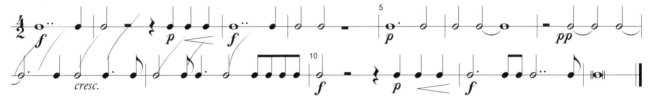

More challenging one-part exercises

147

Allegro

HYPERMETER

What is it that distinguishes an extraordinary composer (or instrumentalist, vocalist, or conductor) from an ordinary one? Among other things, finer musicians are aware of the bigger picture—in particular, higher relationships among beats and measures, pitch motives and phrases. Beyond mastering accuracy of rhythm, they are aware that adjacent beats and measures can form coherent units in music.

Such coherent units may be found in the third movement of Wolfgang Amadeus Mozart's Piano Concerto No. 17 in G Major, K. 453. Each set of four measures creates the aural impression of one stressed beat followed by three less-stressed beats. The duration of each beat would, then, be a whole note.

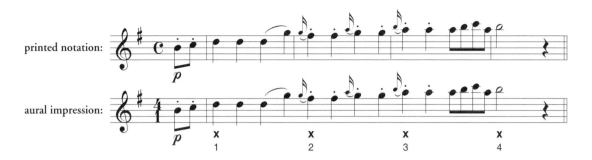

This larger rhythmic organization is known as *hypermeter*. In the example above, four printed measures create a larger unit, which we call a "hypermeasure."

Near the beginning of Ludwig van Beethoven's Fifth Symphony, we hear quadruple meter with a half-note beat:

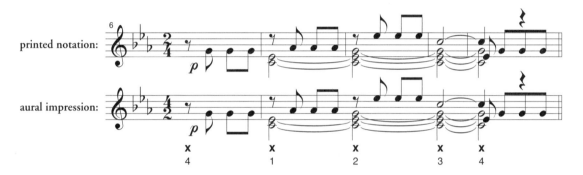

Many Western folk songs also illustrate hypermeter at several levels. Sing "Yankee Doodle" using the three different beat units shown below.

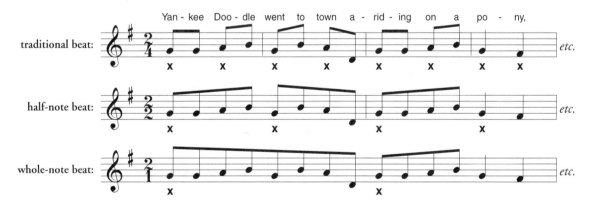

To experience the concept of hypermeter, sing the following songs using progressively larger beat units. For example, sing "Jingle Bells" in $\frac{2}{4}$. Then sing it again while tapping only every other beat, in groups of four, to create $\frac{4}{2}$ meter. Next tap every fourth beat, again in groups of four, to create $\frac{4}{1}$ meter.

▸ "Jingle Bells" (in E♭ major, start on G), refrain:

$\frac{2}{4}$ Jin - gle bells, jin - gle bells, jin - gle all the way,...
    x   x   x   x   x   x   x   x x

▸ "Rock-a-Bye Baby" (in G major, start on B):

$\frac{3}{4}$ Rock - a - bye ba - by, on the tree top,...
    x   x   x x x x x x   x   x x x

▸ "Hickory Dickory Dock" (in C major, start on E):

$\frac{6}{8}$ Hick - o - ry dick - o - ry dock,...
    x   x   x x

148
Andante

Perform this exercise in $\frac{2}{2}$, counting one half-note beat per measure. Each pair of measures forms one hypermeasure.

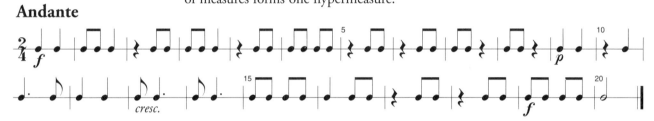

Two-part exercises for one person

149
Andante

150

Andante

Ensemble exercises

151

Allegro

DIMINUTION CANON   The following exercise is a *diminution canon:* The lower line is the same as the upper, except that all the rhythmic values have been divided in half. (Compare this to exercise 96, which is an augmentation canon.)

152

Andante (Diminution Canon)

153

Andante (Canon)

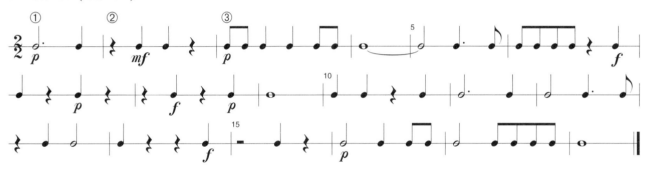

Review exercise

154

Allegretto

Self-test on written concepts

1. On a five-line staff, write a double whole note and a double whole rest.

2. What is an alternate term for "double whole note"?

3. "𝄵" indicates what time signature?

4. What is a "diminution canon"?

5. Circle the two rhythms below that sound identical.

6. Rewrite the following rhythms using tremolo notation:

   a.   =   b.    =

7. Add an appropriate time signature to the measure below. The half note is the beat unit.

8. Circle the measure(s) below with the incorrect number of beats.

9. Indicate the location of each beat with an "**x**" (or a vertical line). The half note is the beat unit.

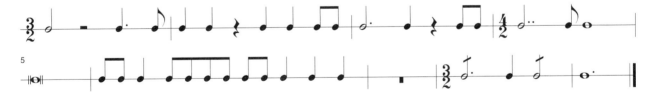

10. Write and perform two rhythm exercises incorporating the rhythmic notation introduced in this chapter.

a. Write and perform an exercise using each of the following at least once:

b. Write and perform an exercise using each of the following at least once:

6

COMPOUND METER: DOTTED HALF-NOTE BEAT

Equivalent cells

This chapter, based on the dotted half-note beat, reintroduces cells first presented in Chapters 2 and 4 with a dotted quarter-note beat. For example, $\frac{6}{8}$ ♪♪♪♪♪♪. ‖ now appears as $\frac{6}{4}$ ♩♩♩♩♩♩ ♩. ‖ .

Worksheet No. 11
Equivalent Cells: Compound Meter, $\frac{x}{8} \longrightarrow \frac{x}{4}$

Rewrite each of the following lines of rhythm using a dotted half-note beat. In your new version, indicate the location of each beat with an "**x**" (or a vertical line).

One-part exercises

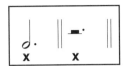 

155

Preparatory drill

156

Allegro

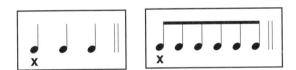

157

Preparatory drill

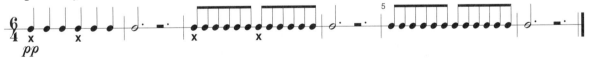

158

Allegro

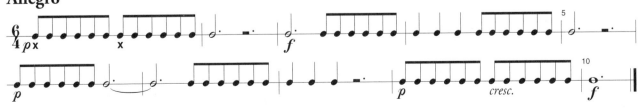

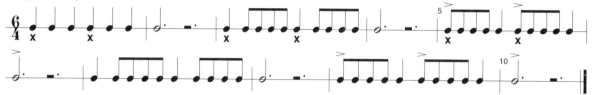

159

Preparatory drill

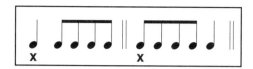

160

Andante

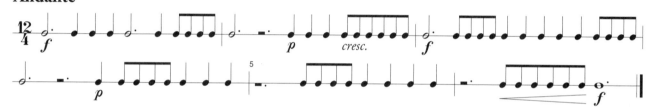

161

Preparatory drill

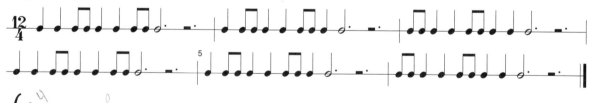

162

Andante

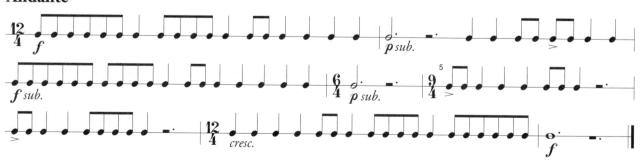

171

Preparatory drill

172

Moderato

173

Preparatory drill

174

Count one beat per measure.

Allegro

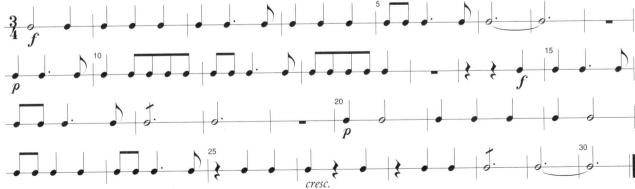

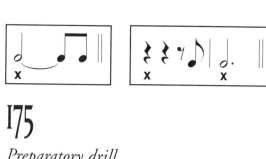

175

Preparatory drill

176

Moderato

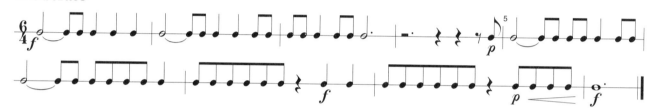

More challenging one-part exercises

177

Count one beat per measure.

Allegro

HYPERMETER   The concept of hypermeter was introduced in Chapter 5 (page 74) in simple meter. Hypermeter is especially relevant to the present chapter because many compositions in $\frac{3}{4}$, such as minuets, waltzes, or scherzos often feature metric relationships suggesting compound duple or quadruple meter. The Menuetto from Franz Joseph Haydn's Symphony No. 94 ("Surprise") suggests $\frac{12}{4}$:

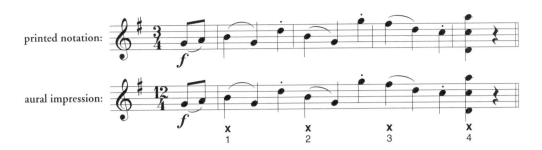

printed notation:

aural impression:

In the second movement of Ludwig van Beethoven's Ninth Symphony, the composer himself indicates hypermeter. Together, the tempo and time signature (Molto vivace, $\stackrel{.}{\downarrow}$ = 116, $\frac{3}{4}$) show that the meter is compound, with one dotted half note per measure. In measure 177, however, Beethoven writes *Ritmo di tre battute* ("rhythm of three beats [i.e., measures]"), thus suggesting three-beat hypermeasures:

printed notation:

aural impression:

Later, in measure 234, Beethoven writes *Ritmo di quattro battute* ("rhythm of four beats"), thus indicating four-beat hypermeasures. Similarly, most of the movement (including the beginning) gives the aural impression of hypermeter, in particular a feeling of $\frac{12}{4}$.

178

Perform this $\frac{3}{4}$ exercise in $\frac{6}{4}$.

Allegretto

Two-part exercises for one person

179

Count one beat per measure.

Adagio

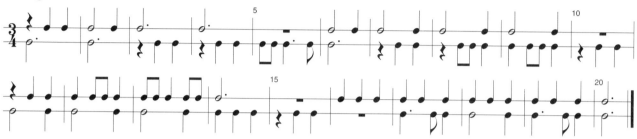

180

Allegro

Ensemble exercise

181

Allegro

Review exercises

182

Count three beats per measure.

Allegretto

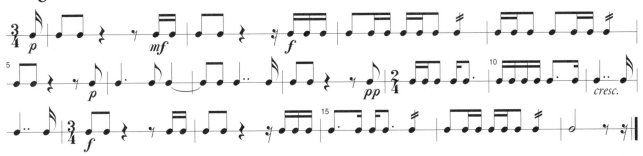

183

Moderato

184

Allegretto

Self-test on written concepts

1. Rewrite the following measured tremolo using non-tremolo notation:

2. Add an appropriate time signature to the measure below (dotted half-note beat).

3. Below, circle the measure(s) with the incorrect number of beats.

4. The following line of music is beamed incorrectly. Renotate the entire line, using beams to join notes within the beat whenever possible.

5. Indicate the location of each beat with an "**x**" (or a vertical line). The dotted half note is the beat unit.

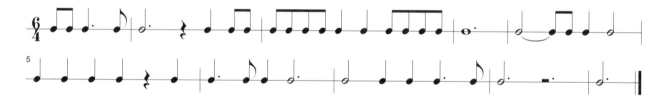

6. Write and perform two rhythm exercises incorporating the rhythmic notation introduced in this chapter.

   a. Write and perform an exercise using each of the following at least once:

   b. Write and perform an exercise using each of the following at least once:

7

SIMPLE METER: EIGHTH-NOTE BEAT

Equivalent cells

This chapter, based on the eighth-note beat, reintroduces cells first presented in Chapters 1 and 3 with a quarter-note beat. For example, $\frac{2}{4}$ ♫♫♩ now appears as $\frac{2}{8}$ ♫♫♪ .

Worksheet No. 12
Equivalent Cells: Simple Meter, $\frac{x}{4} \rightarrow \frac{x}{8}$

Rewrite each of the following lines of rhythm using an eighth-note beat. In your new version, indicate the location of each beat with an "**x**" (or a vertical line).

One-part exercises

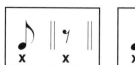 

185

Conduct four beats per measure.

Allegro

At slow tempos in meters such as $\frac{2}{4}$, $\frac{3}{4}$, and $\frac{4}{4}$, it is quite common for composers to indicate a divided beat. For example, in $\frac{2}{4}$, a composer may indicate the tempo as "♪ = 80," and a conductor could then conduct in four. In the remainder of this chapter, many exercises will be included in $\frac{2}{4}$, $\frac{3}{4}$, and $\frac{4}{4}$ in which the direction will be to "tap eighth notes." Such is the case in the exercise below. Even so, continue to be aware of the quarter-note beat.

 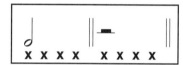

186

Andante

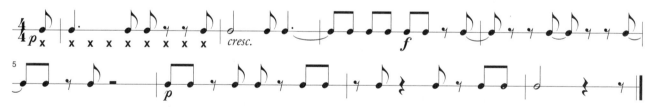

187

Four thirty-second notes (♬♬) are equivalent to one eighth note.

Preparatory drill

188

Allegretto

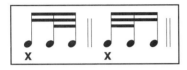

189

Tap eighth notes.

Andante

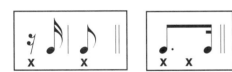

190

Allegretto

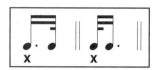

191

Moderato

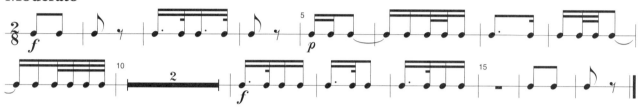

192

Andante

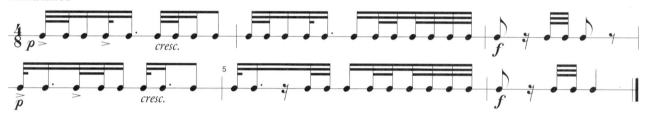

193

Tap eighth notes.

Preparatory drill

194

Tap eighth notes.

Andante

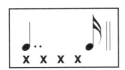

195

Preparatory drill

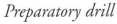

196

Tap eighth notes.

Allegro

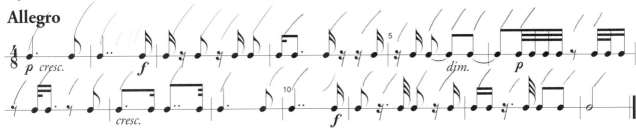

More challenging one-part exercises

♪=♪ The notation "♪=♪" means, literally, *the speed of the new eighth note equals the speed of the old eighth note.*

197

Tap eighth notes throughout this exercise.

Allegro

198

Tap eighth notes throughout.

Andante

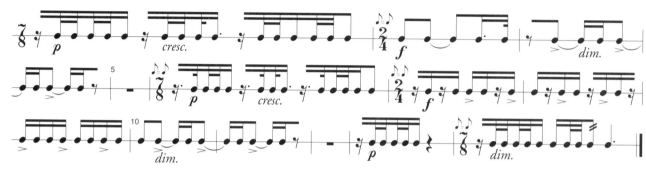

Two-part exercises for one person

199

Adagio

200

Adagio (Canon)

Ensemble exercises

201

Tap eighth notes.

Allegro

202

Tap eighth notes.

Allegretto (Canon)

203

This ensemble exercise uses hocket (see pages 23–24). Tap the beat.

Allegro (Ensemble)

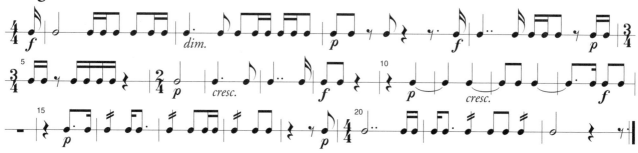

Review exercises

204

Conduct four beats per measure.

Allegro

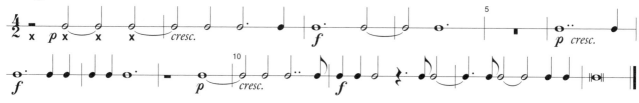

205

Allegro

206

Allegro

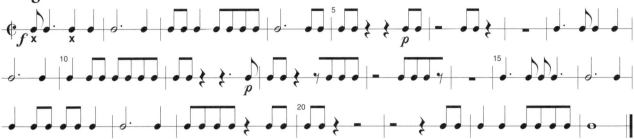

207

Allegro (Ensemble)

208

Allegretto

Self-test on written concepts

1. What does "♪=♪" mean?

2. Below, circle the measure(s) with the incorrect number of beats.

3. Indicate the location of each beat with an "**x**" (or a vertical line). The eighth note is the beat unit.

4. Write and perform two rhythm exercises incorporating the rhythmic notation introduced in this chapter. Beams should join notes within the beat whenever possible.

a. Write and perform an exercise using each of the following at least once:

b. Write and perform an exercise using each of the following at least once:

 and tremolo

COMPOUND METER: DOTTED EIGHTH-NOTE BEAT

Equivalent cells

This chapter, based on the dotted eighth-note beat, reintroduces cells first presented in Chapters 2 and 4 with a dotted quarter-note beat. For example, $\frac{6}{8}$ ♫♫♫♩. ‖ now appears as $\frac{6}{16}$ ♫♫♫♪ ‖ .

Worksheet No. 13
Equivalent Cells: Compound Meter, $\frac{x}{8} \longrightarrow \frac{x}{16}$

Rewrite each of the following lines of rhythm using a dotted eighth-note beat. In your new version, indicate the location of each beat with an "**x**" (or a vertical line).

One-part exercises

209

Preparatory drill

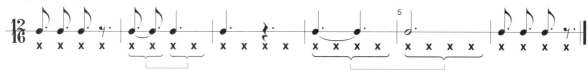

210

Allegro

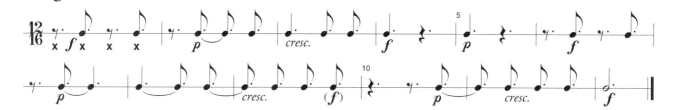

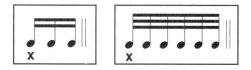

211

Preparatory drill

212

Adagio

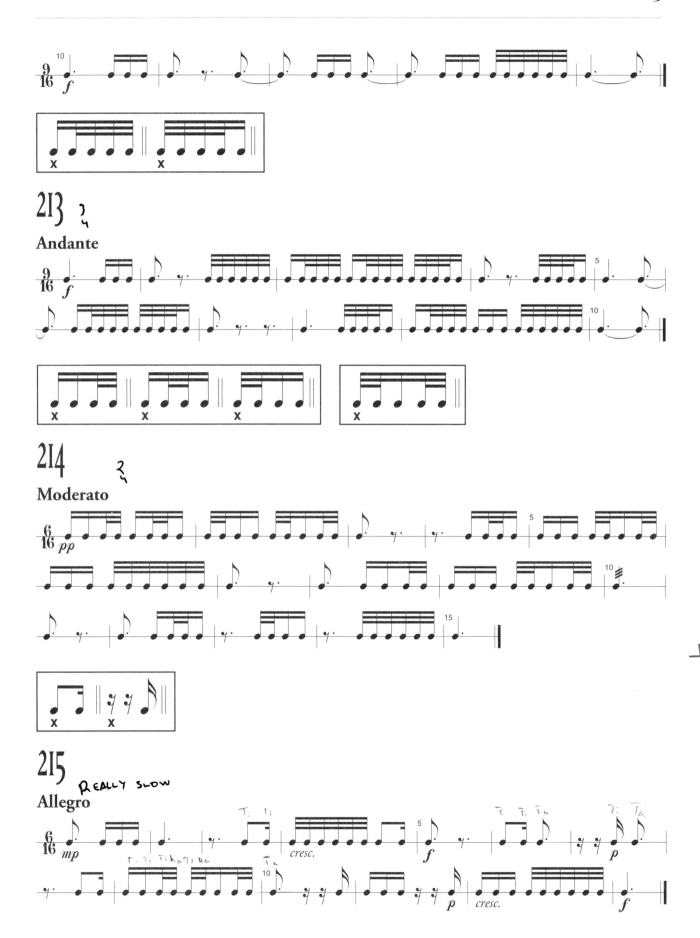

216

Allegro

217

Andante

218

Preparatory drill

219

Count one beat per measure.

Allegro

220

Preparatory drill

221

Moderato

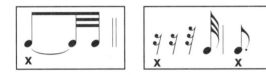

222

Preparatory drill

223

Count one beat per measure.

Allegro

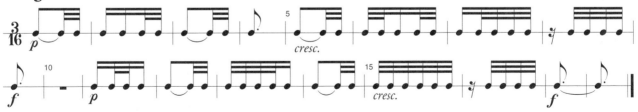

More challenging one-part exercise

224

Moderato

Ensemble exercise

225

Moderato (Canon)

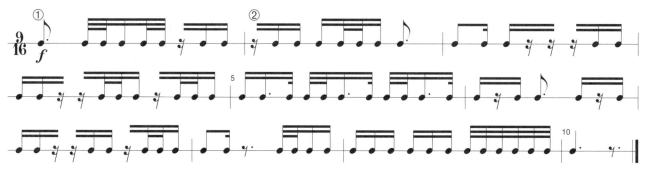

Review exercises

226

Allegretto

227

Allegro

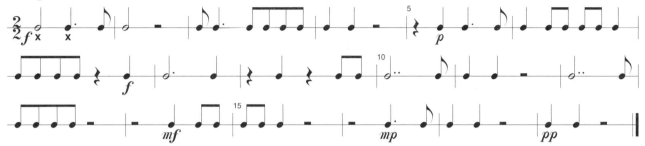

228

Presto

229

Tap eighth notes.

Allegro

230

Count one beat per measure.

Presto

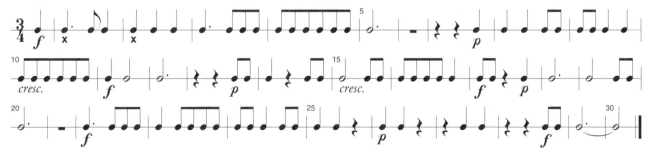

Self-test on written concepts

1. The following line of music is beamed incorrectly. Renotate the entire line, using beams to join notes within the beat whenever possible.

2. Indicate the location of each beat with an "**x**" (or a vertical line). The dotted eighth note is the beat unit.

3. Write and perform two rhythm exercises incorporating the rhythmic notation introduced in this chapter.

   a. Write and perform an exercise using each of the following at least once:

   b. Write and perform an exercise using each of the following at least once:

Irregular Division of the Beat

SimpLe meter:
ALL beat vaLues

Introduction to irregular division of the beat

In simple meter, most rhythm patterns divide the beat into two equal parts.
Further division is also by two. Frequently, however, you will encounter
rhythm patterns that divide the beat not into two (or four, eight, sixteen, and
so forth) parts but into three, five, six, seven, or another number of parts. This
is known as *irregular division of the beat.* The following table illustrates both
regular and irregular division of the beat in simple meter. Irregular division
appears in bold-faced type.

Notes per beat	Number of beams	Example
2	1	
3 (triplet)	1	
4	2	
5 (quintuplet)	2	
6 (sextuplet)	2	
7 (septuplet)	2	
8	3	

We can see that triplets used in $\frac{2}{4}$ resemble eighth notes in $\frac{6}{8}$:

The division into three has, so to speak, been "borrowed" from $\frac{6}{8}$. This type of irregular division, therefore, is also known as *borrowed division*.

Study the beaming in the table above. As you already know, two beams are used for four notes per beat. As the table illustrates, two beams are also used for five, six, and seven notes per beat. (Only when we reach eight notes per beat do we change to *three* beams.) As a rule of thumb, an irregular division of the beat uses the same number of beams as the next smaller *regular division*. For example, seven notes per beat uses two beams—the same as four notes per beat, which is the next smaller regular division.

The notation of irregular division is, however, far from standardized. A triplet, for example, may be notated in any one of the following ways:

The notation is determined by the composer or the publisher. Occasionally, it is not standardized even within a single published music score. For example, in the fourth movement of Maurice Ravel's *Rapsodie espagnole* (Durand, 1908), the following two rhythms appear:

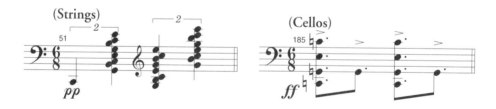

These measures sound rhythmically identical (two notes in the space of a dotted quarter-note beat) but are notated differently. In Igor Stravinsky's *Petrushka* (Russischer Musikverlag, 1912), different rhythms are printed with identical notation in the same measure! (Fourth Tableau, "Dance of the Nursemaids," four measures after rehearsal number 99; tremolos have been deleted.) The upper notes (oboe) are twice as fast as the lower notes (violas):

In the first movement of Maurice Ravel's *Shéhérazade: Trois poèmes pour chant et orchestre* (Durand, 1914), identical rhythms are printed with different notation in adjacent measures:

In both measures, four notes of equal duration (first as eighth notes and then as sixteenth notes) are used to fill one dotted quarter-note beat.

You will need to be flexible when you encounter irregular division in the music you perform and study. Examine the entire measure and the other instrumental or vocal parts as you interpret passages that include irregular division of the beat. In the exercises below, the single most common and correct notation is used.

Quarter-note beat

One-part exercises

TRIPLETS · In simple meter, division of the beat into three notes of equal value constitutes irregular division of the beat. The three notes together are called a *triplet*. The first cell of this unit consists of triplet eighth notes.

231

Preparatory drill (recommended speech cue: "Bee-tho-ven")

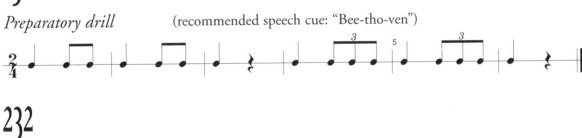

232

Preparatory drill

233
Moderato

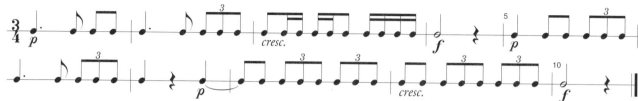

234
Moderato

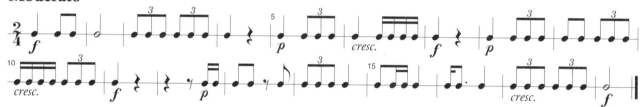

235
Allegro

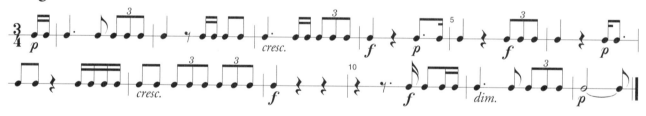

QUINTUPLETS   Performing a *quintuplet* can be quite a challenge. Be sure that the five notes are of equal duration.

236

Preparatory drill   (recommended speech cue: "hip-po-po-ta-mus" or "1-2-3-4-5")

237
Preparatory drill

238
Andante

239
Moderato

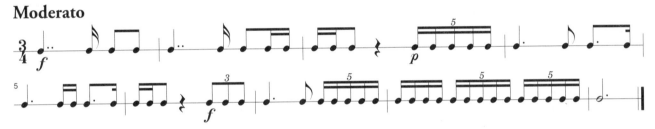

SEXTUPLETS

A *sextuplet*, also known as a sextolet, may be performed as six equally stressed notes. Or it may be performed in two other ways:

1. As two groups of three notes each:	2. As three groups of two notes each:
This creates *simple* division of the beat:	This creates *compound* division of the beat:
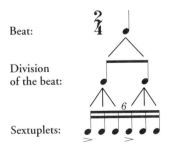	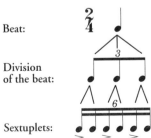

Beat:

Division of the beat:

Sextuplets:

Beat:

Division of the beat:

Sextuplets:

The manner of performance (i.e., how to group the notes) is usually left to the performer's discretion. You will probably find it most natural to perform sextuplets as follows:

1. Perform two groups of three notes when a sextuplet appears next to notes with simple division:

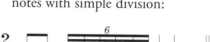

2. Perform three groups of two notes when a sextuplet appears next to notes with compound division:

In either case, the accents should be virtually inaudible.

Worksheet No. 14
Sextuplets

In each of the following measures, rewrite the sextuplets to show the most likely manner of performance. Show note groupings with accents.

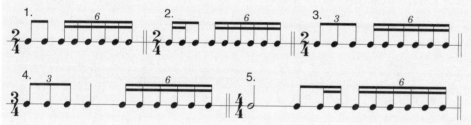

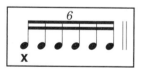

The accents shown below are essential for successful performance. They serve to show how the notes of the sextuplet are grouped.

240

Preparatory drill   (recommended speech cue: "Bee-tho-ven Bee-tho-ven")

241

Andante

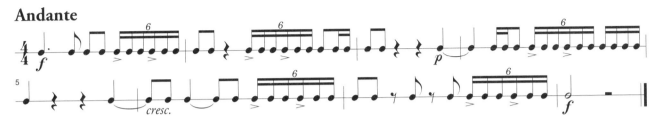

242

Preparatory drill   (recommended speech cue: "ti-kee ti-kee ti-kee")

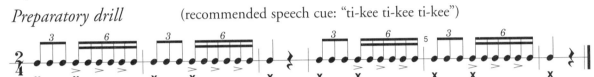

243

Andante

244

Andante

Perform this exercise twice, first with speech cues for all of the sextuplets, and then without speech cues. Be sure to choose the correct speech cue for each sextuplet.

245

Moderato

In this exercise, say "ta" for each note.

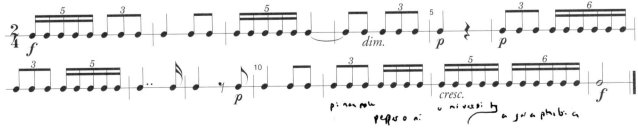

SEPTUPLETS   Choose a fairly slow tempo when performing an exercise that includes a *septuplet.*

246

Preparatory drill   (recommended speech cue: "cir-cum-na-vi-ga-tio-nal" or "1-2-3-4-5-6-7"*)

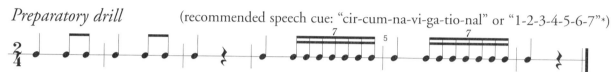

247

Preparatory drill

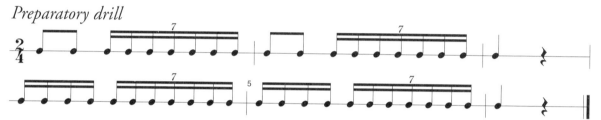

248

Adagio

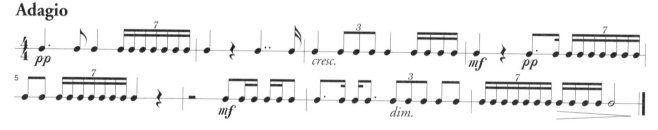

IRREGULAR DIVISION
WITH MEASURED
TREMOLO   Measured tremolo notation is frequently used with irregular division of the beat. The number of slashes represents the number of beams and the Arabic numeral indicates the number of divisions, as illustrated below.

---

*For "7," say "sev."

249

Tap the beat.

Andante

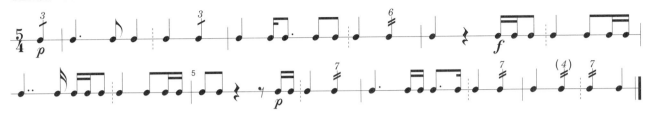

More challenging one-part exercise

250

Allegretto

Two-part exercise for one person

251

Adagio

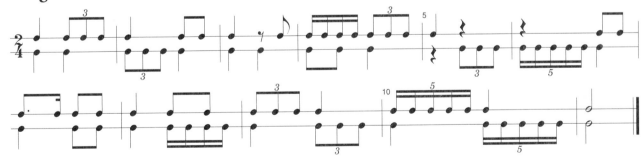

Ensemble exercise

Allegro

Half-note beat

This section, based on the half-note beat, reintroduces cells first presented earlier in the chapter with a quarter-note beat. For example, $\frac{2}{4}$ now appears as $\frac{2}{2}$.

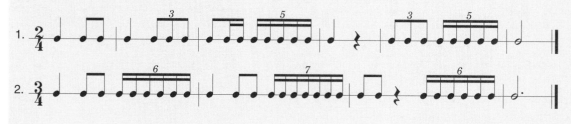

Worksheet No. 15
Equivalent Cells: Simple Meter, $\frac{x}{4} \longrightarrow \frac{x}{2}$

Rewrite each of the following lines of rhythm using a half-note beat. In your new version, indicate the location of each beat with an "**x**" (or a vertical line).

One-part exercises

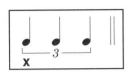 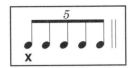

253

Allegro

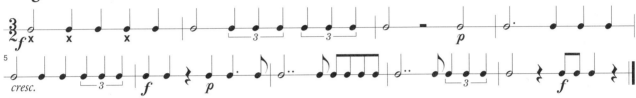

254

Allegretto

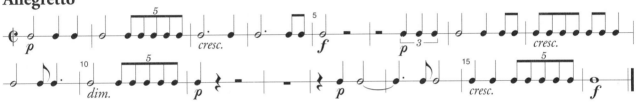

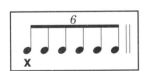 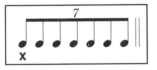

255

Andante

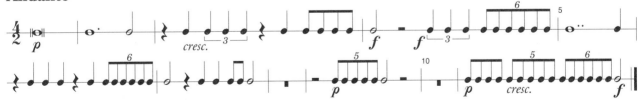

256

Adagio

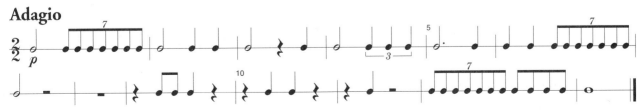

More challenging one-part exercise

257

Use a metronome when practicing this exercise.

Allegretto

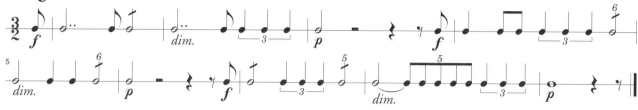

Two-part exercise for one person

258

Adagio

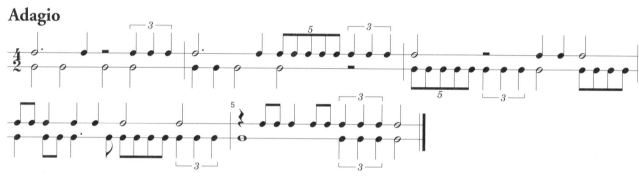

Ensemble exercise

259

Allegro

Eighth-note beat

This section, based on the eighth-note beat, reintroduces cells first presented earlier in the chapter with a quarter-note beat. For example,
now appears as .

Worksheet No. 16
Equivalent Cells: Simple Meter, $\frac{x}{4} \rightarrow \frac{x}{8}$

Rewrite each of the following lines of rhythm using an eighth-note beat. In your new version, indicate the location of each beat with an "**x**" (or a vertical line).

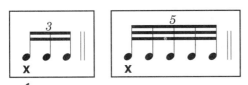

One-part exercises

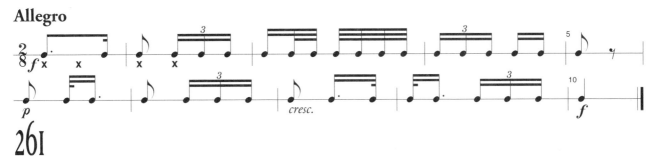

260

Allegro

261

Allegretto

262

Adagio

More challenging one-part exercise

263

Tap the beat.

Adagio

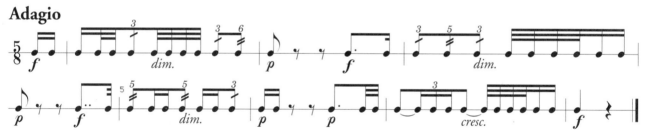

Two-part exercise for one person

264

Adagio

Review exercises

265

Andante

266

Allegro

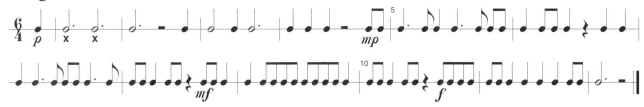

Self-test on written concepts

1. Write a short definition of irregular division of the beat as it applies to simple meter.

2. Fill in the blanks:

   a. Notes that divide the beat into three equal parts form a _____ .

   b. Notes that divide the beat into five equal parts form a _____ .

   c. Notes that divide the beat into six equal parts form a _____ .

   d. Notes that divide the beat into seven equal parts form a _____ .

3. Give two additional ways of notating the following triplet:

4. A sextuplet can be performed as six equally stressed notes. It may also be performed in two other ways.

   a. Describe these two performance options.

   b. How do you know which performance option to choose?

5. Using measured tremolo, write a quintuplet in $\frac{4}{4}$ with the total duration of a quarter note.

6. Add bar lines to the following two lines of rhythm.

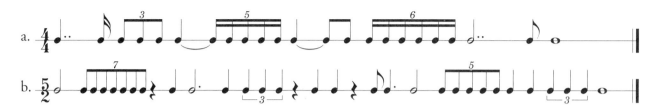

7. Write and perform three rhythm exercises incorporating the rhythmic notation introduced in this chapter.

a. Write and perform an exercise using a quarter-note beat. Use each of the following at least once:

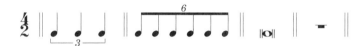

b. Write and perform an exercise using a half-note beat. Use each of the following at least once:

c. Write and perform an exercise using an eighth-note beat. Use each of the following at least once:

COMPOUND METER: ALL BEAT VALUES

Irregular division of the beat in compound meter

In compound meter, the beat is usually divided into three equal parts. Further division is by two. The beat in compound meter may also be divided into two, four, five, seven, or some other number of parts. This constitutes irregular division of the beat. In the table below, irregular division appears in bold-faced type.

Notes per beat	Number of beams	Example
2 (duplet)	1	
3	1	
4 (quadruplet)	1	
5 (quintuplet)	1	
6	2	
7 (septuplet)	2	

Compare regular and irregular division of the beat in compound meter (above) with that in simple meter (see page 111).

Dotted quarter-note beat

One-part exercises

DUPLETS In compound meter, a *duplet* indicates the appearance of two notes (rather than three) in the space of one beat. A duplet may be notated in a variety of ways:

When performing duplets, be sure to maintain a steady tempo. Use a metronome when practicing the exercises below.

267

Preparatory drill   (recommended speech cue: "ba-ker")

268

Preparatory drill

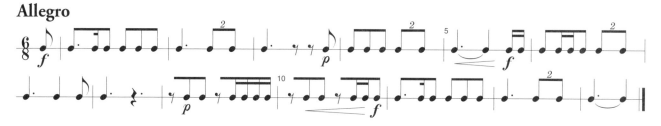

269

Allegro

270

Allegro

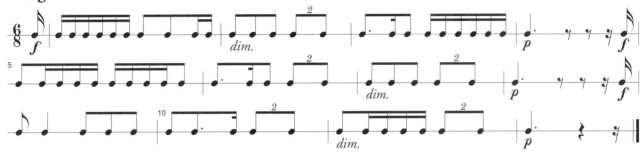

QUADRUPLETS   The *quadruplet* in compound meter (see the cell box below) reveals an idiosyncrasy of rhythmic notation. Even though it is performed twice as fast, a quadruplet has the same number of beams.

271

Preparatory drill   (recommended speech cue: "pea-nut but-ter")

272

Preparatory drill

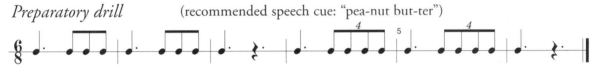

273

Andante

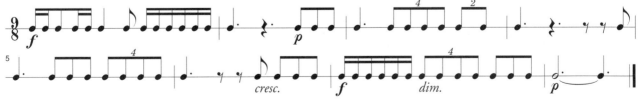

274

Andante

QUINTUPLETS   Perform the notes of a *quintuplet* as evenly as possible. Be sure that the five notes are of equal duration.

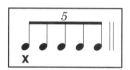

275

Preparatory drill   (recommended speech cue: "hip-po-po-ta-mus" or "1-2-3-4-5")

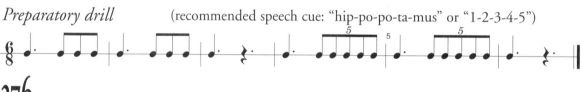

276

Preparatory drill

277

In this exercise, count one beat per measure.

Allegro

SEPTUPLETS   When an exercise includes a *septuplet,* choose a tempo that is slow enough to allow you to perform the notes successfully.

278

Preparatory drill   (recommended speech cue: "cir-cum-na-vi-ga-tio-nal" or "1-2-3-4-5-6-7"*)

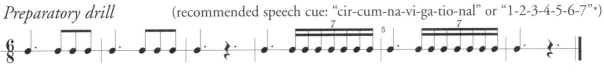

279

Preparatory drill

280

Andante

More challenging one-part exercise

281

In this exercise, measures 6–9 may "feel" like simple meter.

Allegro

*For "7," say "sev."

Two-part exercise for one person

282

Allegro

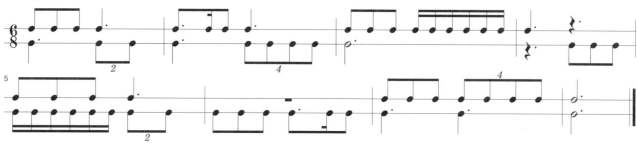

Ensemble exercise

283

Andante

Dotted half-note beat

This section, based on the dotted half-note beat, reintroduces cells first presented earlier in the chapter with a dotted quarter-note beat. For example, $\frac{6}{8}$ now appears as $\frac{6}{4}$.

Worksheet No. 17
Equivalent Cells: Compound Meter, $\frac{x}{8} \longrightarrow \frac{x}{4}$

Rewrite each of the following lines of rhythm using a dotted half-note beat. In your new version, indicate the location of each beat with an "**x**" (or a vertical line).

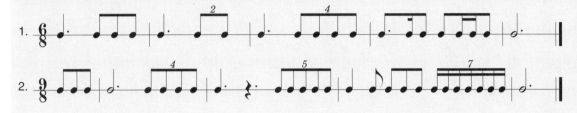

One-part exercises

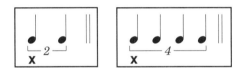

284

Preparatory drill

285

Preparatory drill

286

Count one beat per measure.

Allegro

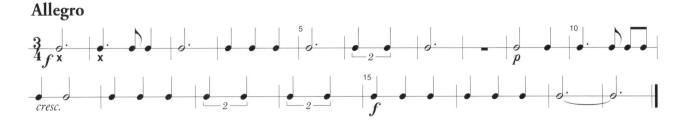

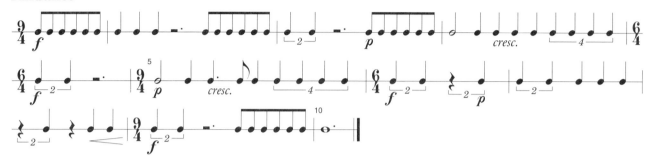

287

Andante

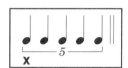

288

Preparatory drill

289

Mark the location of each beat.

Andante

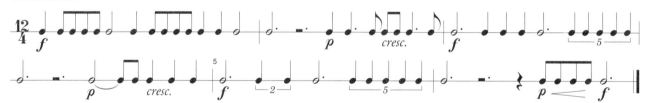

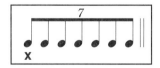

290

Preparatory drill

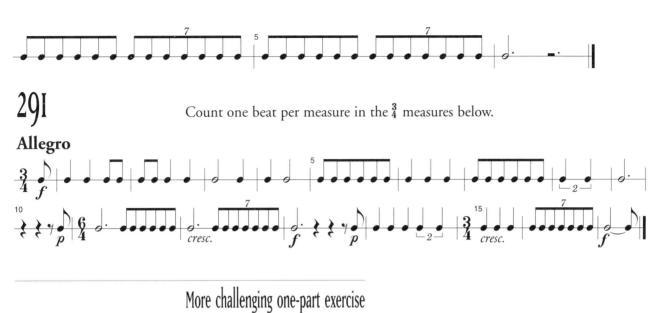

291

Count one beat per measure in the $\frac{3}{4}$ measures below.

Allegro

More challenging one-part exercise

292

Add your own dynamics.

Allegro

Two-part exercise for one person

293

Andante

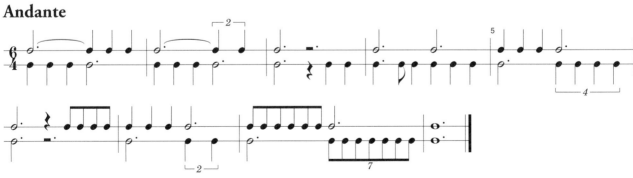

Ensemble exercise

294

Allegro

Dotted eighth-note beat

This section, based on the dotted eighth-note beat, reintroduces cells first presented earlier in the chapter with a dotted quarter-note beat. For example, $\frac{6}{8}$ ♫ ♩. ‖ now appears as $\frac{6}{16}$ ♫ ♪. ‖ .

Worksheet No. 18
Equivalent Cells: Compound Meter, $\frac{x}{8}$ → $\frac{x}{16}$

Rewrite each of the following lines of rhythm using a dotted eighth-note beat. In your new version, indicate the location of each beat with an "**x**" (or a vertical line).

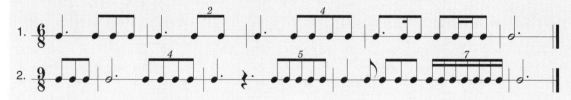

One-part exercises

295

Count one beat per measure.

Allegro

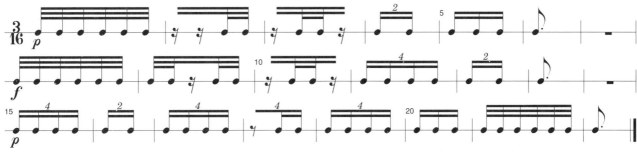

296

Andante

Ensemble exercise

297

Adagio (Canon)

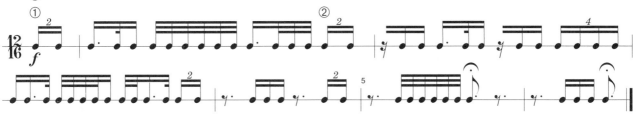

Review exercises

298

Allegro

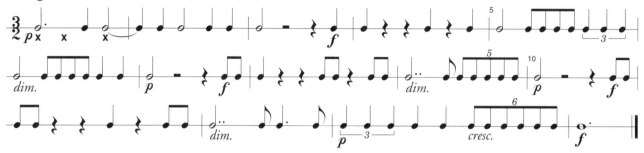

299

Tap eighth notes.

Adagio

Self-test on written concepts

1. Fill in the blanks:

    a. Notes that divide the beat into two equal parts form a _____ .

    b. Notes that divide the beat into four equal parts form a _____ .

2. Add bar lines to the following line of rhythm:

3. Rewrite the following rhythms using tremolo notation:

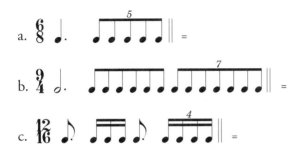

4. Write and perform three rhythm exercises incorporating the rhythmic notation introduced in this chapter.

   a. Write and perform an exercise using a dotted quarter-note beat. Use each of the following at least once:

   b. Write and perform an exercise using a dotted half-note beat. Use each of the following at least once:

   c. Write and perform an exercise using a dotted eighth-note beat. Use each of the following at least once:

Syncopation

Simple meter: Quarter-note beat

Introduction to syncopation

In the most general sense, *syncopation* is a "momentary contradiction of the prevailing meter or pulse."* Syncopation occurs when an accent is placed on a traditionally unstressed beat or unstressed part of a beat, as illustrated below.

a. Accent on an unstressed beat:

b. Accent on an unstressed part of a beat:

We also perceive such an accent on a note that follows a rest or a tied note that ends on a beat or a stressed part of a beat.

a. Accent on an unstressed beat:

b. Accent on an unstressed part of a beat:

*Don Michael Randel, ed., *The New Harvard Dictionary of Music* (Cambridge, Mass.: Belknap Press of Harvard University Press, 1986).

In order for syncopation to be perceived as such, a regular pattern of stressed and unstressed beats and divisions of the beat must be established before the syncopation occurs, or, alternatively, such a pattern must be audible at the same time the syncopated pattern is heard.

You have already performed numerous exercises with syncopation throughout chapters 1–8; many of these exercises included syncopation at the level of the *beat* (see, for example, exercises 54, 57, 90, 92, 118, and 147). In Chapters 11–13 you will perform exercises with syncopation that occurs at the level of the *division of the beat.*

In music, accents can be used to reinforce the normal stress of a beat or they can be used to create syncopation. Several types of accents may occur. In his book *Principles of Rhythm,* Paul Creston lists no fewer than nine different types!* The most important of these are the following six:

1. *Dynamic accent.* A note or chord that is louder than nearby notes or chords:

4. *Pitch accent.* The highest or lowest pitch of a melodic pitch pattern:

2. *Agogic accent.* A note or chord that is longer than surrounding notes or chords:

5. *Pattern accent.* The first pitch of a repeated pitch pattern:

3. *Harmonic accent.* A dissonant chord that is in the midst of relatively consonant chords:

6. *Embellished accent.* A note with melodic embellishment (such as a trill):

For examples of syncopation in printed music, see exercises 399, 400, 401, 402, 407, 410, 417, 422, and 426 in Chapters 14–16. For singing and listening at this time, a list of music with syncopation appears at the end of this chapter.

---

*Paul Creston, *Principles of Rhythm* (New York: Franco Colombo, 1964) pp. 28–33.

One-part exercises

300

Preparatory drill

301

Moderato

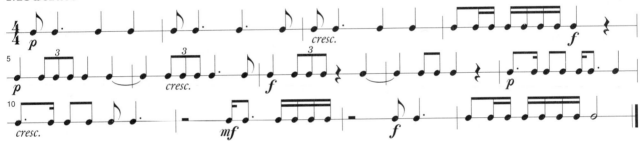

302

Allegretto

303

Preparatory drill

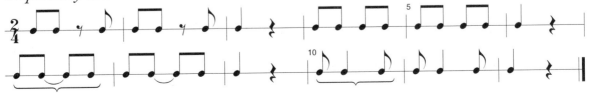

304

Allegro

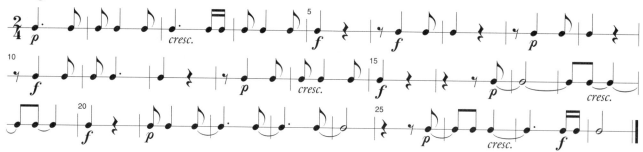

305

Mark the location of each beat in this exercise.

Andante

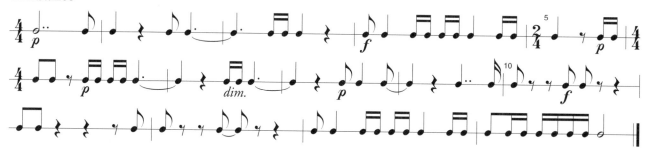

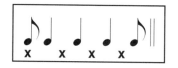

In this cell, every beat except the first is obscured.

306

Preparatory drill

307

Mark the location of each beat.

Moderato

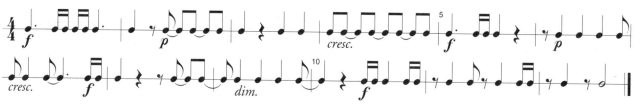

308

Allegro

Tap the beat.

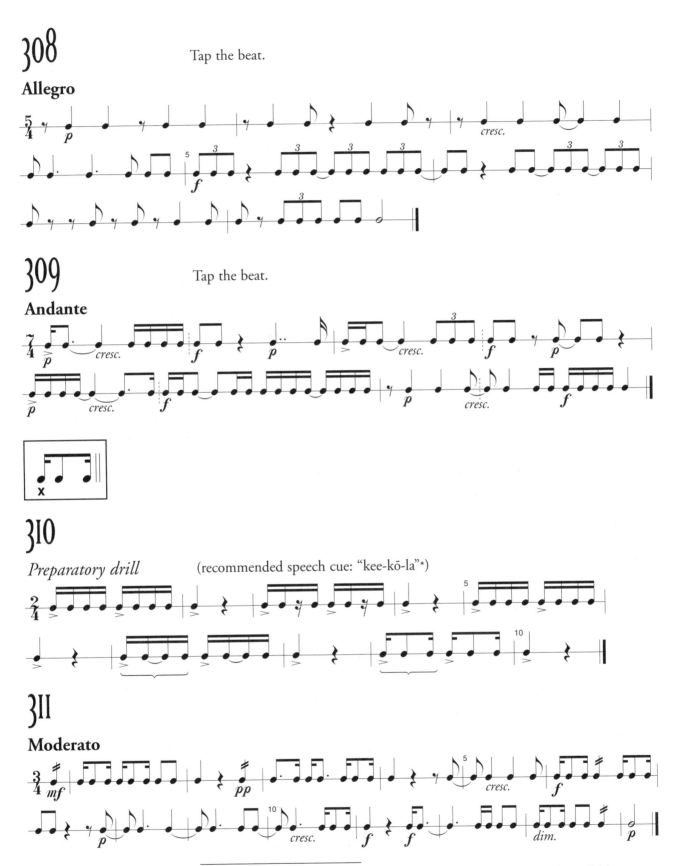

309

Andante

Tap the beat.

310

Preparatory drill (recommended speech cue: "kee-kō-la"*)

311

Moderato

*Place an accent on "kee." Hold the syllable "kō" longer than the other syllables.

312

Andante

CROSS RHYTHMS:
SUPERDUPLET

The rhythm cells presented in the remainder of this chapter are known as *cross rhythms.* The first, called a *superduplet,* is colloquially referred to as "two against three." In $\frac{3}{4}$, a superduplet may be notated in several different ways:

When you encounter a superduplet, regardless of the notation you see, recall the version listed first in the patterns above. (Note that it is also listed first in the cell box below.) This version is the easiest to read because it is a rhythm pattern you have already seen frequently. The only addition is the tie between notes two and three.

All five versions notated above are identical in sound. The second version, which is a shorthand for the first, is identical in appearance to a measure in $\frac{6}{8}$:

313

Preparatory drill

314

Moderato

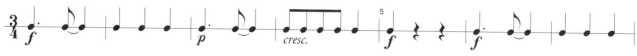

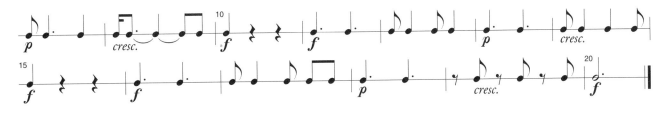

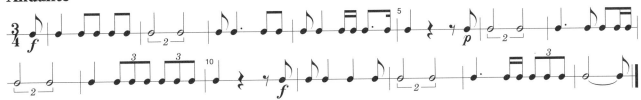

315

Andante

316

Allegretto

SUPERTRIPLET   A *supertriplet*, or "three against two" (three notes in the space of two beats), can also be notated in more than one way, as shown in the cell box below.

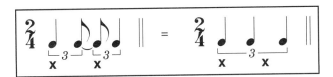

317

Preparatory drill

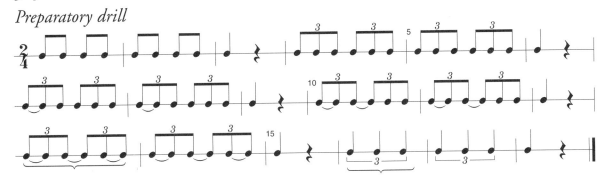

318

Andante

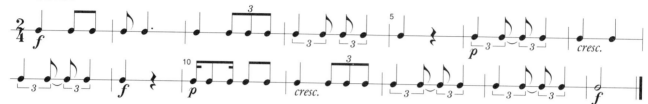

319

Adagio

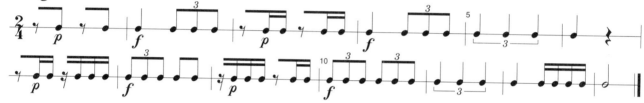

LESS COMMON CROSS RHYTHMS

The superduplet and supertriplet appear frequently in music. Such patterns as *"four against three," "three against four,"* and *"two against five"* are less common. The preparatory drills below will assist you in learning these unusual patterns.

"FOUR AGAINST THREE"

In this pattern, four notes are performed in the space of three beats.

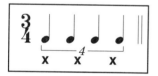

320

Preparatory drill

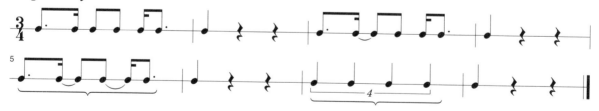

"THREE AGAINST FOUR"   In this pattern, three notes are performed in the space of four beats.

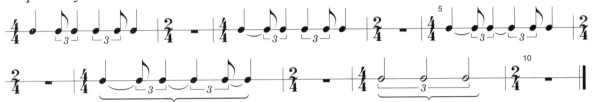

321

Preparatory drill

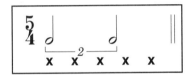

"TWO AGAINST FIVE"   In this pattern, two notes are performed in the space of five beats.

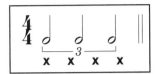

322

Tap the beat.

Preparatory drill

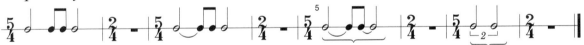

More challenging one-part exercise

323

Moderato

Two-part exercises for one person

324
Preparatory drill

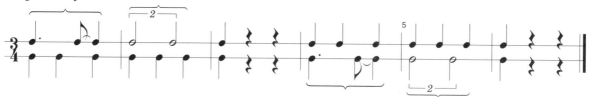

325
Andante

326
Preparatory drill

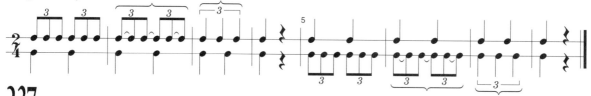

327
Andante

Ensemble exercise

328

Allegro

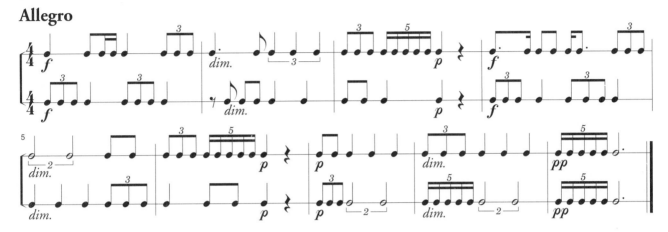

Review exercises

329

Andante

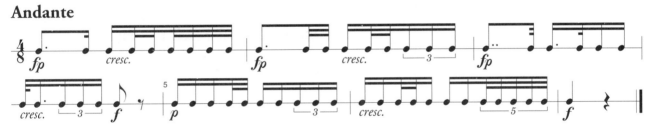

330

Allegro

Self-test on written concepts

1. Write a line of rhythm using syncopation, incorporating an accent both on a traditionally unstressed *beat* and on a traditionally unstressed *part of a beat*.

2. Write six examples of accent, one in each of the categories below. Refer to (but do not copy) the examples given on page 144.

   a. Dynamic accent.

   b. Agogic accent.

   c. Harmonic accent.

   d. Pitch accent.

   e. Pattern accent.

   f. Embellished accent.

3. Circle examples of syncopation in each line of rhythm:

4. Give an alternate notation for each of the following cells:

5. "Three against four" refers to three _____ in the space of four _____ .

6. Indicate the location of each beat with an "**x**" (or a vertical line). The quarter note is the beat unit.

7. Write and perform a rhythm exercise incorporating the rhythmic notation introduced in this chapter. The quarter note is the beat unit. Use each of the following at least once:

Recommended listening

The following songs include syncopated rhythm patterns:

- Frank Campbell/Billy Reeves, "Shoo, Fly, Don't Bother Me"

- Daniel Emmett, "Dixie"

- Stephen Foster, "Camptown Races"

- Meredith Willson, *The Music Man:* "Goodnight Ladies"

The beginning of each movement below features syncopation.

- Johann Sebastian Bach, Keyboard Concerto in D Minor, BWV 1052: first movement (Allegro)

- Johann Sebastian Bach, Keyboard Concerto in F Minor, BWV 1056: first movement (Allegro)

- Béla Bartók, Rumanian Folk Dances: first movement (Joc Cu Bâtă)

- Ludwig van Beethoven, Sonata for Piano and Cello in A Major, Op. 69: second movement (Scherzo: Allegro molto)

- Ludwig van Beethoven, Sonata for Violin and Piano in A Major, Op. 47 ("Kreutzer"): second movement (Andante con variazioni)

- Leonard Bernstein, *Trouble in Tahiti:* Prelude

- Antonin Dvořák, Symphony No. 9 in E Minor, Op. 95 ("From the New World"): first movement (Adagio; Allegro molto)

- Scott Joplin, *Maple Leaf Rag* and *Elite Syncopations*

- Darius Milhaud, *La création du monde:* second movement (Fugue)

- Wolfgang Amadeus Mozart, Symphony No. 40 in G Minor, K. 550: third movement (Menuetto: Allegro)

- Igor Stravinsky, *Le sacre du printemps:* "Dances des adolescentes"

For comparison, the following music does *not* use syncopation:

- Johann Sebastian Bach, Brandenburg Concerto No. 3 in G Major, BWV 1048: first movement

- Franz Joseph Haydn, Concerto in E♭ for Trumpet and Orchestra: first movement (Allegro)

COMPOUND METER: ALL BEAT VALUES

Dotted quarter-note beat

Perform each exercise in this chapter twice: first without ties, then as written.

One-part exercises

331

Andante

HEMIOLA   *Hemiola* is a type of syncopation in which three notes of equal value appear in the space of two beats. The meter appears to change from $\frac{6}{8}$ to $\frac{3}{4}$ or from $\frac{6}{4}$ to $\frac{3}{2}$, as shown in the two examples below.

Compare this to the supertriplet in simple meter (page 149).

Hemiola appears frequently in the music of the Renaissance and Baroque, as well as in the music of such Romantic-era composers as Robert Schumann (1810–1856) and Johannes Brahms (1833–1897). Several examples of hemiola appear below, each marked by a dotted oval.

▸ Claudio Monteverdi, *Orfeo*, Act II, Ritornello. Opening measures:

▸ Robert Schumann, Symphony No. 3 in E♭ Major ("Rhenish"), Op. 97: first movement (Lebhaft). Hemiola across the bar line (one beat per measure). Opening measures:

▸ Johann Strauss, *Blue Danube Waltz:* Waltz No. 3. Hemiola across the bar line (one beat per measure). Opening measures:

▸ Maurice Ravel, *Alborada del gracioso.* Opening measures:

332

Preparatory drill

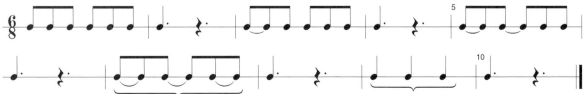

Allegro

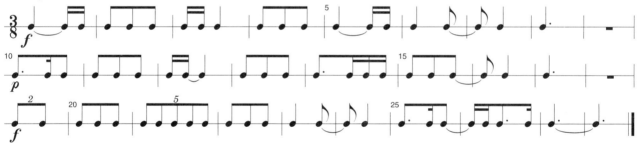

335
Allegro

Count one beat per measure.

More challenging one-part exercise

336
Allegretto

Mark the location of each beat in measures 3 and 4. Perform this exercise first without ties, and then again adding the ties.

Two-part exercises for one person

337

Preparatory drill

338

Andante

Ensemble exercise

339

Allegro

Dotted half-note beat

This section, based on the dotted half-note beat, reintroduces cells first presented earlier in the chapter with a dotted quarter-note beat. For example,

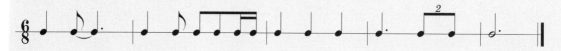

now appears as

Worksheet No. 19
Equivalent Cells: Compound Meter, $\frac{x}{8} \rightarrow \frac{x}{4}$

Rewrite each of the following lines of rhythm using a dotted half-note beat. In your new version, indicate the location of each beat with an "**x**" (or a vertical line).

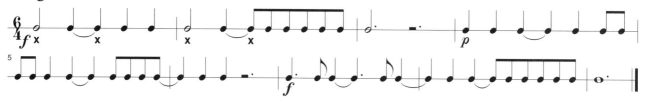

One-part exercises

340
Allegro

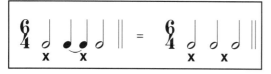

341
Preparatory drill

In the exercises below, each set of quarter-note duplets and quarter-note quadruplets fills one dotted half-note beat.

342
Allegro

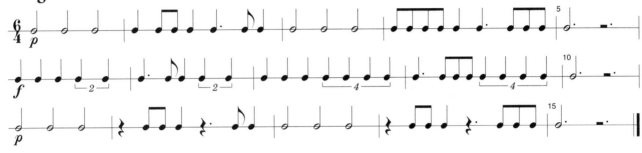

More challenging one-part exercise

343
Moderato

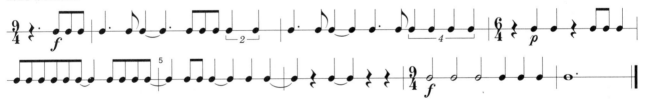

Two-part exercises for one person

344
Preparatory drill

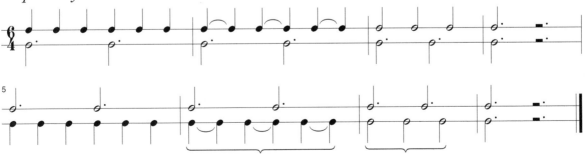

345
Andante

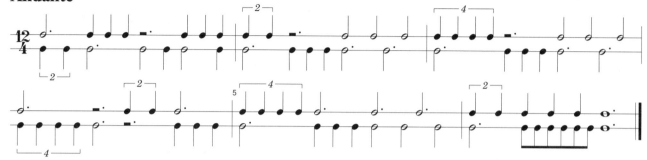

Dotted eighth-note beat

This section, based on the dotted eighth-note beat, reintroduces cells first presented earlier in the chapter with a dotted quarter-note beat. For example, $\frac{6}{8}$ ♩ ♩ ♩ ‖ now appears as $\frac{6}{16}$ ♫♪ ‖.

Worksheet No. 20
Equivalent Cells: Compound Meter, $\frac{x}{8} \rightarrow \frac{x}{16}$

Rewrite each of the following lines of rhythm using a dotted eighth-note beat. In your new version, indicate the location of each beat with an "**x**" (or a vertical line).

- - -

One-part exercises

346
Allegro

Count one beat per measure.

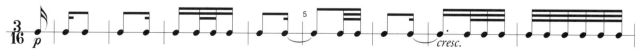

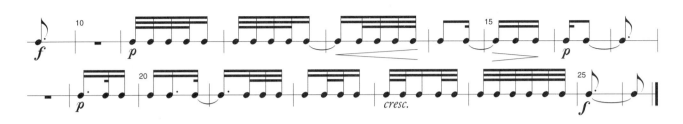

347

Preparatory drill

348

Adagio

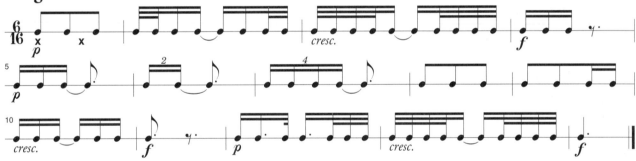

Two-part exercises for one person

349

Preparatory drill

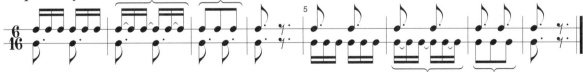

350
Andante

Ensemble exercise

351
Allegro

Review exercise

352
Allegro (Ensemble)

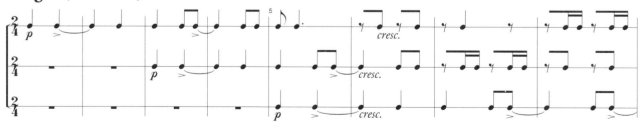

Self-test on written concepts

1. Give an alternate notation for each of the following cells:

a. $\quad$ **6/8** $\quad \bullet \quad \bullet \quad \bullet \quad \| \quad =$

b. $\quad$ **6/4** $\quad \bullet \quad \bullet \quad \bullet \quad \| \quad =$

c. $\quad$ **6/16** $\quad \bullet\bullet\bullet \quad \| \quad =$

2. What is meant by "hemiola"?

3. Add bar lines and indicate the location of each beat:

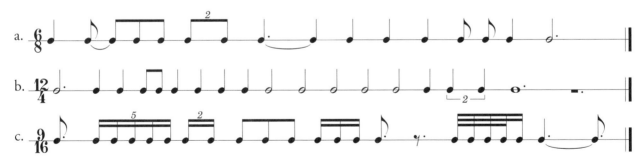

4. Write and perform three rhythm exercises incorporating the rhythmic notation introduced in this chapter:

   a. Write and perform an exercise using a dotted quarter-note beat. Use each of the following at least once:

b. Write and perform an exercise using a dotted half-note beat. Use each
of the following at least once:

c. Write and perform an exercise using a dotted eighth-note beat. Use
each of the following at least once:

13

Simple meter;
Half-note beat;
Eighth-note beat

Half-note beat

This section, based on the half-note beat, reintroduces cells first presented in Chapter 11 with a quarter-note beat. For example, $\frac{2}{4}$ ♪ ♪ ♩ ♪ ‖ now appears as $\frac{2}{2}$ ♩ 𝅗𝅥 ♩ ‖.

Worksheet No. 21
Equivalent Cells: Simple Meter, $\frac{x}{4} \longrightarrow \frac{x}{2}$

Rewrite each of the following lines of rhythm using a half-note beat. In your new version, indicate the location of each beat with an "**x**" (or a vertical line).

One-part exercises

353

Preparatory drill

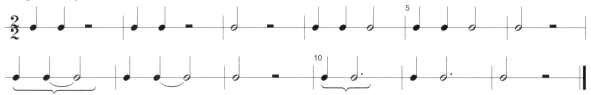

354

Allegretto

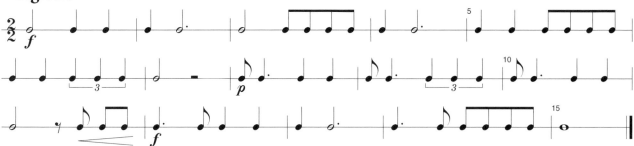

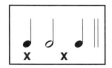

355

Preparatory drill

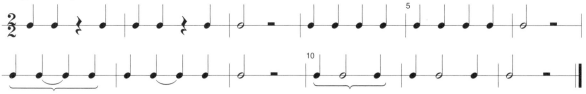

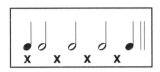

356

Preparatory drill

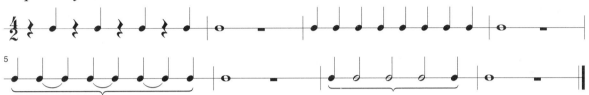

357

Moderato

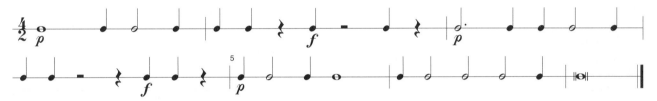

358

Andante

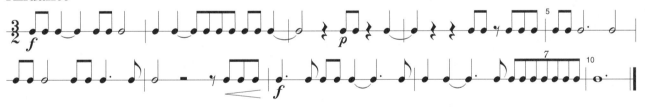

359

Preparatory drill

360

Allegro

361

Preparatory drill

362

Adagio

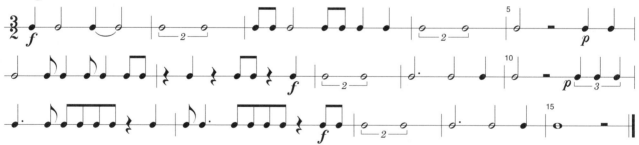

363

Allegro

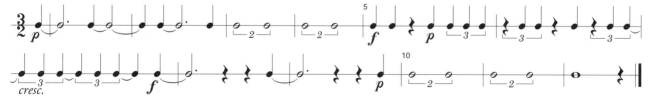

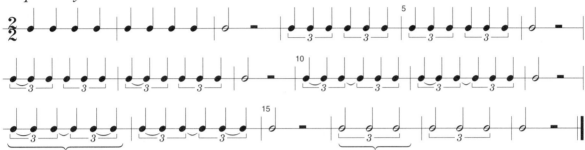

364

Preparatory drill

365

Adagio

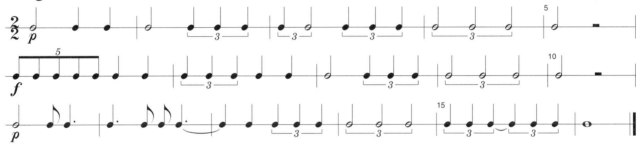

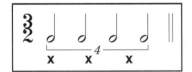

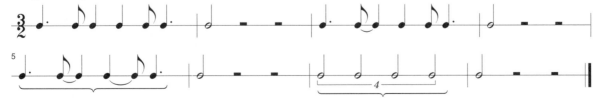

366

Preparatory drill

367

Preparatory drill

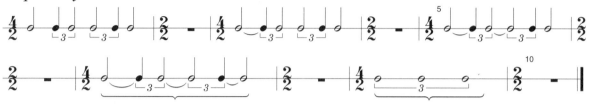

368

Preparatory drill

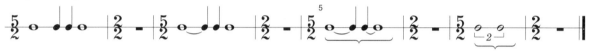

More challenging one-part exercise

369

Allegro

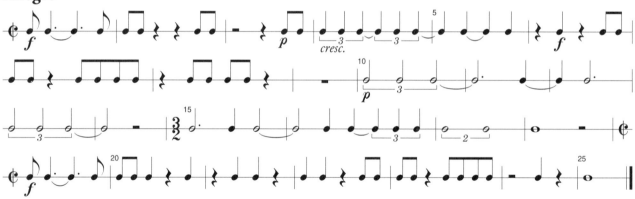

Two-part exercises for one person

370

Preparatory drill

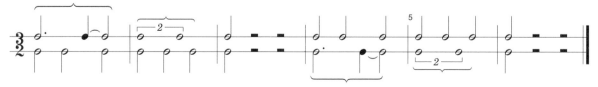

371

Adagio

372

Preparatory drill

373

Adagio

Ensemble exercise

374

Allegro (Canon)

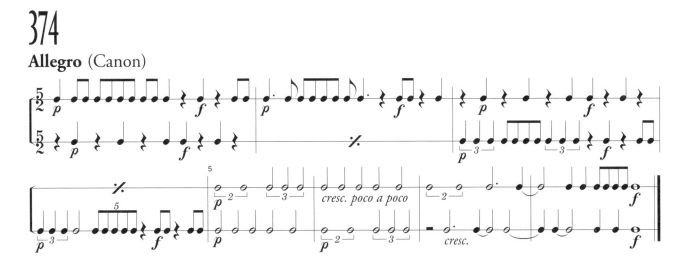

Eighth-note beat

This section, based on the eighth-note beat, reintroduces cells first presented in Chapter 11 with a quarter-note beat. For example,  now appears as .

Worksheet No. 22
Equivalent Cells: Simple Meter, $\frac{x}{4} \rightarrow \frac{x}{8}$

Rewrite each of the following lines of rhythm using an eighth-note beat. In your new version, indicate the location of each beat with an "**x**" (or a vertical line).

One-part exercises

375

Preparatory drill

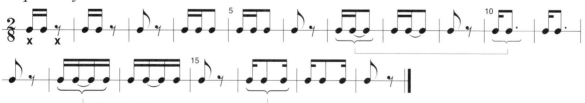

376

Allegro

377

Preparatory drill

378

Mark the location of each beat in the first two lines of this exercise.

Andante

379

Moderato

380

Preparatory drill

381

Andante

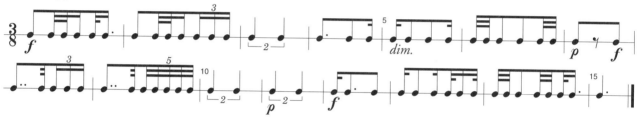

382

Preparatory drill

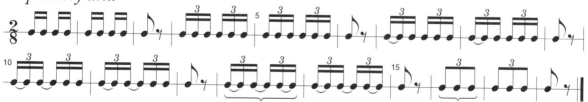

383

Adagio

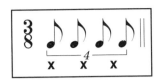 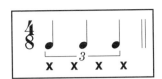 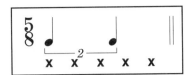

384

Preparatory drill

385

Preparatory drill

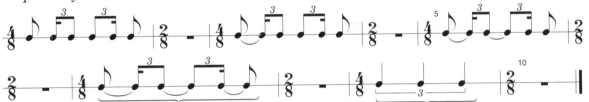

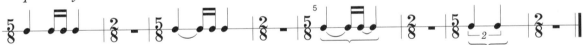

386

Preparatory drill

More challenging one-part exercise

387

Allegro

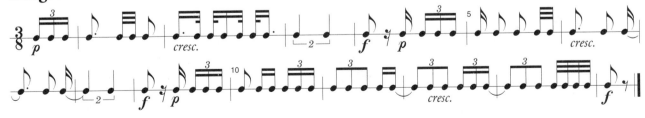

Two-part exercises for one person

388

Preparatory drill

389

Andante

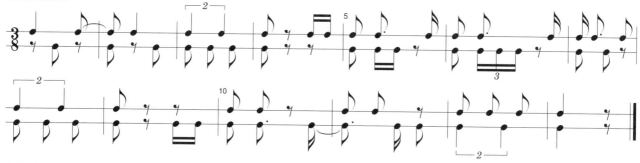

390

Preparatory drill

391

Andante

Ensemble exercises

392

Tap the beat.

Allegro

393

Andante (Canon)

Review exercises

394

Allegro

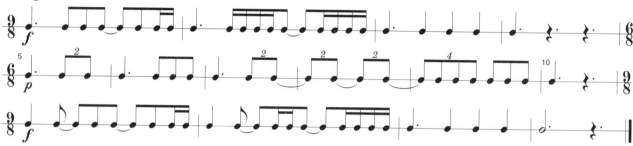

395

Andante

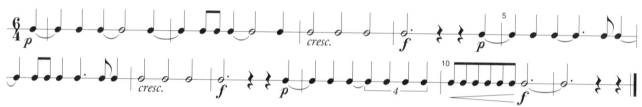

396

Moderato

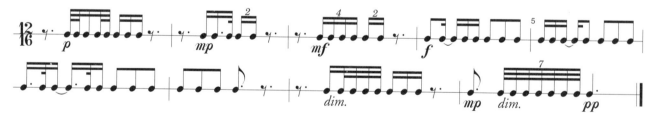

Self-test on written concepts

1. Indicate the location of each beat with an "**x**" (or a vertical line). The half note is the beat unit.

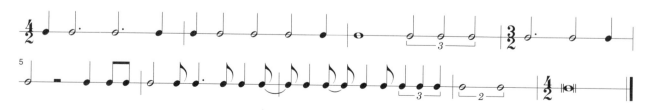

2. Indicate the location of each beat with an "**x**" (or a vertical line). The eighth note is the beat unit.

3. Write and perform two rhythm exercises incorporating the rhythmic notation introduced in this chapter.

a. Write and perform an exercise using a half-note beat. Use each of the following at least once:

b. Write and perform an exercise using an eighth-note beat. Use each of the following at least once:

Excerpts
from
Music
Literature

Excerpts in Traditional Meters

In Chapters 14, 15, and 16, perform only the rhythm element of each excerpt. A glossary of musical terms that appear in these exercises is located at the back of this book.

Excerpts in Chapters 14 and 15 are arranged in order of increasing difficulty.

One-part exercises

397

This excerpt, even though it lacks bar lines and meter, should have a $\frac{3}{8}$ or $\frac{6}{8}$ feel.

Guillaume de Machaut (ca. 1300–1377), *Dame a vous sans retollir*

Dame a vous sans re-tol - lir Dong cuer pen-se-e de-sir Corps et a-mour

398

Circle examples of inverted dotting in this folk song. (See discussion of inverted dotting on page 48.)

Scottish folk song, *Maiden of the Dark Brown Hair*

Nigh-ean dubh 's a nigh-ean donn Shiubhl-ainn leat far m'eòl-ais; Nigh-ean dubh 's a nigh-ean donn.

'S mis - e tha gu mul - a-dach Air m'uil - inn anns an t - seòmb-ar.

399

In this excerpt, count one beat per measure. Locate four examples of hemiola across a bar line. (See discussion of hemiola on pages 156–57.)

Presto

Johann Sebastian Bach (1685–1750), Keyboard Concerto in F Minor, BWV 1056

400

Count one beat per measure.

Ludwig van Beethoven (1770–1827), Symphony No. 3 in E♭ Major ("Eroica"), Op. 55

Allegro con brio ♩. = 60

401

Igor Stravinsky (1882–1971), *Rite of Spring*, "Auguries of Spring" (Dance of the Adolescents)

Tempo giusto ♩ = 56

402

Tranquille ♩ = 96

Darius Milhaud (1892–1974), *Saudades do Brazil*, VII. "Corcovado"

403

Mouvement de Habanera   Claude Debussy (1862–1918), *Estampes,* II. "La soirée dans Grenade"

404   Count one beat per measure.

Allegro con fuoco ♩. = 80   Emmanuel Chabrier (1841–94), *España*

405   Anonymous (fourteenth century), *Caligo terrae scinditur*

Ca - li - go— ter - rae scin - di - tur, Per - cus - sa— so - lis spi - cu - lo,

Dum sol ex— stel - la na - sci - tur, In— fi - de - i di - lu - cu - lo;

406   Leonard Bernstein (1918–90), *Fancy Free*

Very fast four ♩ = 100

411

Animé ♩ = 126   Darius Milhaud (1892–1974), *Le boeuf sur le toit*

Ensemble exercises

RHYTHMIC
ALTERATION IN
BAROQUE MUSIC

When performing music of the Baroque era (ca.1600–1750), important decisions must be made with regard to rhythm. In some cases, printed rhythms cannot be taken literally. Several excellent books discuss these matters in detail.* In performances of Baroque music, dotted notes that appear near triplets are sometimes performed as triplets. For example, [musical notation] may be performed as [musical notation] . Perform exercise 412 in this fashion. For example, the first measure should be performed as follows:

---

*See, for example, Robert Donington, *Baroque Music: Style and Performance, A Handbook* (New York: W. W. Norton, 1982) and Stephen E. Hefling, *Rhythmic Alteration in Seventeenth- and Eighteenth-Century Music* (New York: Schirmer Books, 1993). In particular, you may wish to read their discussions of "double dotting" (intentional over-dotting) and "notes inégales" (performance of equal-value notes as notes of unequal duration).

412

Larghetto

George Frideric Handel (1685–1759),
Sonata in A Minor for Recorder and Continuo, Op. 1, No. 4

413

♩ = 62

Darius Milhaud (1892–1974), *La création du monde*

Study the following two excerpts closely before you begin! Note, for example, that the first measure of the lower voice in exercise 414 appears to have too many beats. In fact, the last half note of that measure is simply a notational shorthand for a quarter note tied *over the bar line* to another quarter note. This method of notation has been employed by present-day musicologists when transcribing Renaissance music.

416

♩ = 135

Elliott Carter (b. 1908), String Quartet No. 1

15

More chaLLenging excerpts in traditional meters

One-part exercises

417

Vivace con brio

Leonard Bernstein (1918–90), *Jeremiah Symphony*

418

Tempo di marcia

Scott Joplin (1868–1917), *Maple Leaf Rag*

419   For this excerpt, remember that ♩♪♪♩ is equivalent to ♩♩♩. In other words, this pattern is "three against two" (three notes in the space of two beats).

Slow, with deep emotion ♩ = 60   Paul Creston (1906–85), Symphony No. 2, Op. 35

420   Matteo da Perugia (late 1300s–early 1400s), *Serà quel zorno*

421

Presto capriccioso alla napolitana ♩ = ca. 88   William Walton (1902–83), Violin Concerto

422

Easy, swingy ♩ = 84   Leonard Bernstein (1918–90), *Trouble in Tahiti*

423

Allegro ♩. = 104

Hector Berlioz (1803–69), *Symphonie fantastique*, Op. 14

424

Corrente

Johann Sebastian Bach (1685–1750), Partita No. 6 in E Minor, BWV 830

425

For this excerpt, remember that $\frac{4}{4}$ ♩—3—♩—3—♩ is equivalent to $\frac{4}{4}$ ♩♩♩. In other words, this pattern is "three against four" (three notes in the space of four beats) or, if performed with two beats per measure, "three against two" (three notes in the space of two half-note beats).

Animado ♩ = 120

Heitor Villa-Lobos (1887–1959), *Canções tipicas brasileiras*, "Xangô"

426   Count one beat per measure.

Allegro ♩ = ca. 138–144   Béla Bartók (1881–1945), *Music for Strings, Percussion, and Celeste*

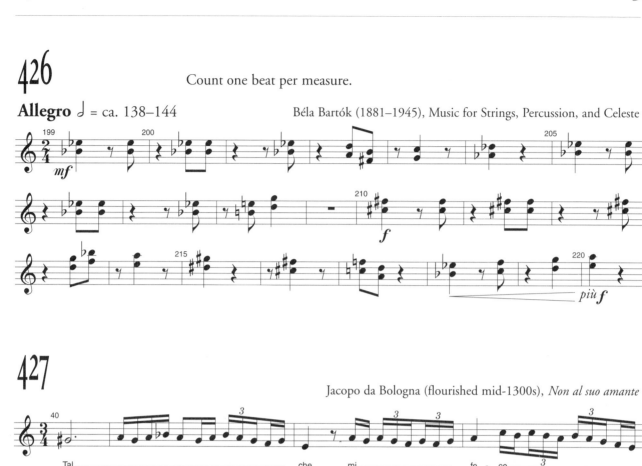

427

Jacopo da Bologna (flourished mid-1300s), *Non al suo amante*

Tal_____ che mi_____ fe - ce_____

quan - do gli ar - de'l_____ cie - - - - - - - - - lo Tu

428

Easy, swingy ♩ = 84   Leonard Bernstein (1918–90), *Trouble in Tahiti*

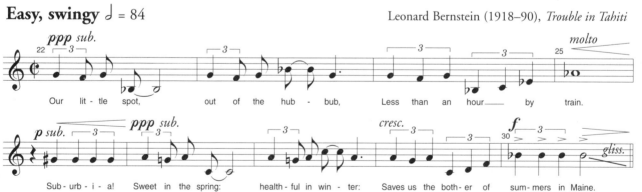

Our lit - tle spot, out of the hub - bub, Less than an hour_____ by train.

Sub - urb - i - a! Sweet in the spring: health - ful in win - ter: Saves us the both - er of sum - mers in Maine.

429

Marsch: Gewichtig ♩ = 104   Paul Hindemith (1895–1963), *Die Harmonie der Welt*

430

♩ = 69   Edgar Varèse (1883–1965), *Ionisation*

431   Count one beat per measure.

Meno allegro ♪ = 138–144   Charles Ives (1874–1954), Symphony No. 4

432

In measure 5, note that $\frac{3}{4}$ ♪ ♪ ♪ ♪ | is equivalent to $\frac{3}{4}$ ♩ ♩ ♩ ♩ |.

Anton Webern (1883–1945), *Five Canons*, Op. 16, No. 3

Langsam ♩ = ca. 50

Crux   fi - de - lis,   in - ter   om - nes   ar - bor   u - na   no - bi - lis:

nul - la   sil - va   ta - lem   pro - fert,

433

Edgar Varèse (1883–1965), *Density 21.5*

♩ = 72

434

When first learning this excerpt, you may wish to tap eighth notes.

Lento molto marcato ♩ = 54

Aaron Copland (1900–90), *Vitebsk*

435

Mark the location of each beat in this exercise.

Allegro fantastico ♩ = 112

Elliott Carter (b. 1908), String Quartet No. 2

436

Tap eighth notes in this excerpt. At first, however, you may even wish to tap sixteenth notes! Before you begin, mark the location of each beat or division of the beat.

Allemande

Johann Sebastian Bach (1685–1750), Suite for Solo Cello in D Major, BWV 1012

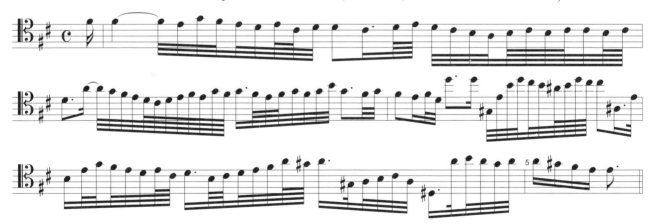

Two-part exercise for one person

Allegretto   Johann Sebastian Bach (1685–1750), Two-Part Inventions, No. 6, BWV 777

Ensemble exercises

438

This excerpt includes hocket (see discussion of hocket on pages 23–24).

Anonymous, *A l'entrade d'avril*

439

Giovanni Pierluigi da Palestrina (ca. 1525–94), *Missa Veni sponsa Christi*, Kyrie

440

This excerpt includes hocket.

Guillaume de Machaut (ca. 1300–77), *Double hoquet*

441 Circle each example of hemiola in this excerpt. (See discussion of hemiola on pages 156–57.)

Guillaume Dufay (ca. 1400–74), *La dolce vista*

442

Allegretto ♩ = 104–108

Heitor Villa-Lobos (1887–1959), *Bachianas Brasileiras No. 5*

Excerpts in Nontraditional Meters

Composite meter

The twentieth century has seen many innovations in music composition and music notation, including the use of nontraditional meters. We have studied one of these, *composite meter*, in Chapter 1 (page 19). In a composite meter, each measure is divided into two or more unequal parts, as the following examples illustrate:

In a slow or moderate tempo, we count or conduct each beat of the measure. In $\frac{5}{4}$, for example, we count five quarter-note beats per measure. In a fast tempo, however, it may not be possible to count each beat. Rather, we count groups of beats, which creates larger beat units that alternate regularly within each measure. In $\frac{5}{8}$, for example, the new beat unit alternates between a quarter note and a dotted-quarter note while the division unit (the eighth note) remains constant:

To indicate this grouping, many composers write the time signature for a composite meter in a fast tempo as follows:

This type of time signature is used for other composite meters as well:

Exercises

Before performing exercises in composite meter, you must first learn to tap or conduct a constantly changing beat unit. Remember that the division unit—unlike the beat unit—remains constant. Practice each of the following exercises twice, at a very fast tempo. First *tap* the beat; then *conduct* the beat. Conduct $\frac{5}{4}$ with a two-beat pattern, elongating one of the beats.

443

Preparatory drill (Ensemble)

444

Presto

445

Preparatory drill (Ensemble)

446

Presto

447
Presto

Use a three-beat conducting pattern for ⅞. In this exercise, elongate the third beat.

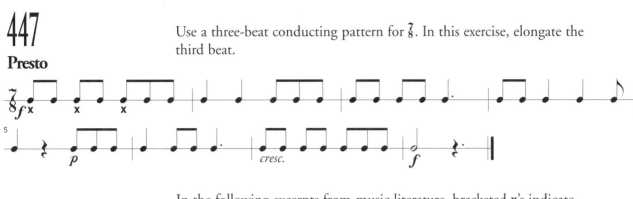

In the following excerpts from music literature, bracketed **x**'s indicate recommended placement of the beats.

448

Count three beats per measure.

Greek folk song, *Dance of Zalongo*

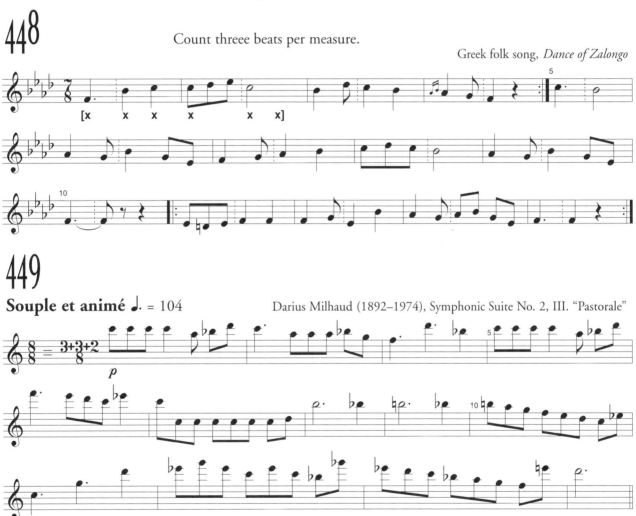

449

Souple et animé ♩. = 104   Darius Milhaud (1892–1974), Symphonic Suite No. 2, III. "Pastorale"

450

Bulgarian folk song, *There's No One Like Gana*

Za - tri - la si Gá - na   kri - vo pé - ro,   kri - vo pé - ro Gá - na,   pa - û - nió - vo,

Gá - chi - tze   le   Gá - no,   pi - le   rá - no,   es   na   gó - re   Gá - no,   es   na   dó - le,

Gán - chi - tze   le   Gá - no,   pi - le   rá - no,   es   na   gó - re   Gá - no,   es   na   dó - le.

451

Bulgarian folk song, *Grief*

Ne   mé   e   zál - ko,   má - le   le,   ché   she   se   o - zé - - ni,

ne   mé   e   zál - ko,   má - le   le,   ché   she   se   o - zé - - ni,

no   me   e   zál - ko,   má - le   le,   ché   bli - zo   doi - dé.

452

Allegretto ♩ = ca. 114   Béla Bartók (1881–1945), Concerto for Orchestra

453

Allegro vivace ♩. = 88

Béla Bartók (1881–1945), Concerto for Orchestra

454

Igor Stravinsky (1882–1971),
Rite of Spring, "Sacrificial Dance (The Chosen One)"

Tempo giusto ♪ = 126

455

Con impeto ♩ = 120

Luigi Dallapiccola (1904–75), *Il prigioniero*

456

♩ = 112

Igor Stravinsky (1882–1971), *L'histoire du soldat*

Double meter

Measure-by-measure alternation between two different meters is indicated with a *double meter*.

Exercises

457

Serbian folk song, *Gine*

When hemiola occurs regularly in music, the composer may notate the music with a double time signature, as shown below. A dotted oval indicates each hemiola. (See additional examples of hemiola on pages 156–57.)

▸ Aaron Copland, *El Salón México*
Rehearsal number 7:

▸ Leonard Bernstein, *West Side Story:* "America"
Tempo di Huapango (fast), mm. 5–8:

I like to be in A - mer - i - ca! O. K. by me in A - mer - i - ca

458

Portugese folk song, *Vines and Girls*

Vi - dei - ri - nha dá - me um ca - cho, Ó ca - cho dá - me um ba - gui - nho. Me -

ni - na dê - me um a - bra - ço, Que eu lhe da - rei um bei - ji - nho.

Unusual beat units

Exercises

In the following excerpts, the beat unit is an unusually small or large note value.

459

(Ensemble)

George Philipp Telemann (1681–1767), Three Duets, "Lilliputsche Chaconne"

LONGA   In the excerpt below, recall that 𝄼 indicates a breve (double whole note). The last note, a *longa*, is equivalent to three tied whole notes, or a dotted double whole note. Composers no longer use this symbol.

460

Giovanni Pierluigi da Palestrina (ca. 1525–94), *Veni sancte Spiritus*

Far more unusual beat units may be found in compositions written in the twentieth century. Unlike the excerpts above, the following three compositions do not lend themselves to in-class performance.

▸ Carl Orff, *Carmina Burana*
  Meters used: $\frac{8}{\circ\cdot}$, $\frac{3}{8}$, $\frac{4}{\text{IOI}}$, and others. "Veris leta facies," measure 6:

▸ Charles Wuorinen, *Bicinium for Two Oboes*
  Meters used: $\frac{1}{32}$, $\frac{11}{64}$, $\frac{20^{3/4}}{8}$, and others. Final measures:

▸ Karlheinz Stockhausen, *Mixtur (Nr. 16½)*
  Meters used: $\frac{1}{\circ\cdot\cdot}$, $\circ\_\frac{1}{\circ}\_\circ$, $\frac{2}{\circ\cdot}+\frac{1}{\circ\cdot}$, and several others. It is necessary to examine an entire page or two of this score. *Mixtur (Nr. 16½)* is readily available in college music libraries.

Metric modulation

Metric modulation (also known as tempo modulation) is the technique of creating a precise, and usually unobtrusive, change in tempo through one or more changes in meter. This technique has been used most notably by Elliott

Carter. Essential to the effect produced, an equivalency is notated in the score indicating that a particular note value (*x*) in the old meter equals a particular note value (*y*) in the new meter: *x* = *y*.

Exercises

461

As an introduction to the concept of metric modulation, first practice the last line of this excerpt.

Elliott Carter (b. 1908), String Quartet No. 1

462

Elliott Carter (b. 1908), Eight Pieces for Four Timpani, "Canaries"

Polymetric music

The ensemble exercises below are *polymetric*: Different voices simultaneously perform in different meters.

Ensemble exercises

463

(Ensemble)

In this excerpt, the speed of the beat in the top line is in a 3:2 relationship with the speed of the beat in the middle and bottom lines.

Johannes Ciconia (ca. 1335–1411), *Sus une fontayne*

464

(Ensemble)

Baude Cordier (flourished ca. 1400), *Amans ames*

The excerpts above were composed around 1400. Polymetric music is much more common in the twentieth century, but it usually appears in shorter passages. The following examples do not lend themselves to in-class performance:

▸ Luigi Dallapiccola, *Sex Carmina Alcaei*
VI. Molto lento, ma senza trascinare:

▸ Béla Bartók, String Quartet No. 2, Op. 17
First movement (Moderato), rehearsal number 8:

Ametric music

Recall the description of meter presented at the beginning of this book: *Meter refers to the organization or pattern of beats and divisions of the beat.* When the listener cannot perceive beats or divisions of the beat, we say the music is *ametric,* even if it includes a printed time signature.

Liturgical chant from the medieval period is usually performed ametrically. Most twentieth-century electronic music is also ametric. In both cases, the listener is unable to discern regular beats or divisions of the beat.

Exercises

465

In this exercise you will perform the last four printed measures of a thirteen-measure composition. The music includes no time signature, and the composer instructs the performers to avoid metrical accents and to make their clapping sounds identical so that the two parts will blend together.

(Ensemble)

♩ = 160–184   Repeat each bar 12 times

Steve Reich (b. 1936), *Clapping Music for Two Performers*

The following examples of ametric music do not lend themselves to in-class performance:

▸ Luciano Berio, *Sequenza I per Flauto Solo*
  Opening:

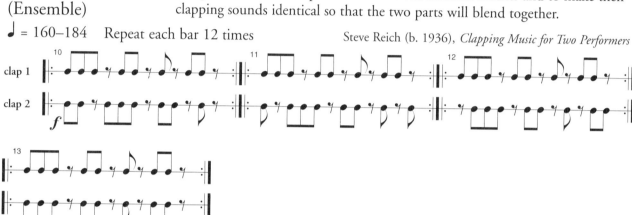

▸ Charles Ives, *The Cage*
  Opening:

back to the oth - er side; he stopped on - ly when the keep - er came a - round with meat;

Review exercise

466

This exercise incorporates many rhythmic concepts, including syncopation and composite meter.

♩ = 152

John Adams (b. 1947), *The Chairman Dances (Foxtrot for Orchestra)*

Self-test on written concepts

1. Write and perform a rhythm exercise using the following double time signature: $\frac{3}{2}\frac{6}{4}$.

2. In $\frac{4}{32}$, what does the "32" mean?

3. In $\frac{13}{8}$, what does the "13" mean?

4. Music that simultaneously uses different meters is called _____ .

5. What is unusual about the beat unit in a composite meter at a fast tempo?

6. Music that lacks a discernible meter is called _____ .

Appendix A

Special rhythmic symbols in twentieth-century music

Twentieth-century composers frequently use special rhythmic symbols in their music. Here is a sampling of the symbols you may encounter:

Notes and stems

ritardando

accelerando

play as fast as possible

$1\frac{1}{4}$ times the value of the note

hold the note for the duration of the line

Holds and pauses

Λ   short hold

     medium hold

     medium pause

     long pause

Conducting patterns

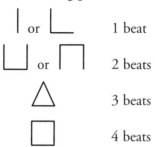

⎮ or ⎣	1 beat
⎵ or ⎴	2 beats
△	3 beats
☐	4 beats

To see some of these symbols used in a music score, examine the following scores while listening to a recording of each work:

- Pierre Boulez, *Improvisation sur Mallarmé*

- George Crumb, *Vox Balaenae (Voice of the Whale)* and *Ancient Voices of Children*

- Krzysztof Penderecki, *Threnody for the Victims of Hiroshima*

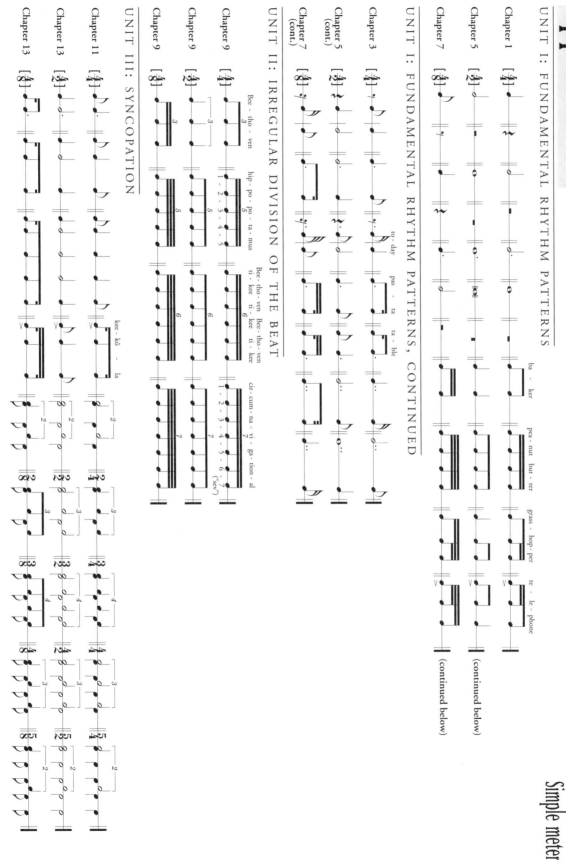

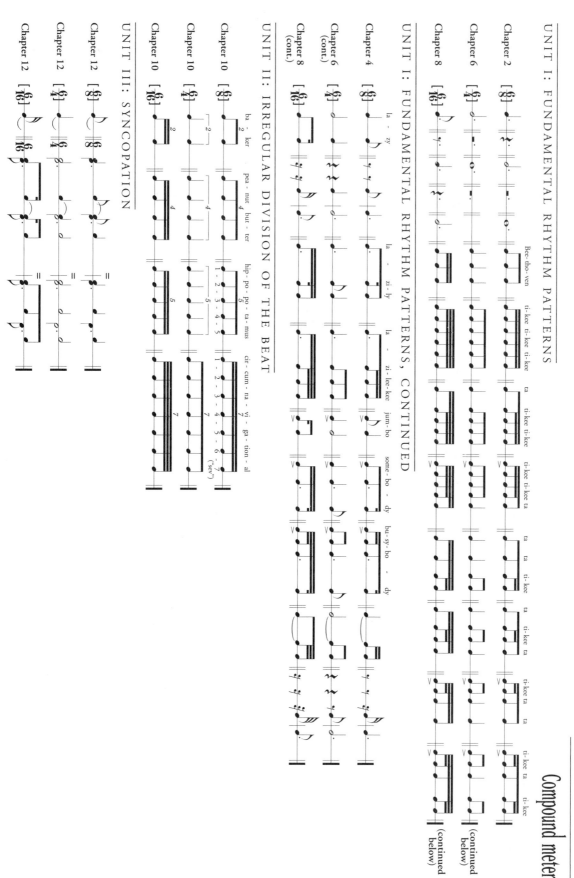

RHYTHM CELLS
Compound meter

UNIT I: FUNDAMENTAL RHYTHM PATTERNS

UNIT I: FUNDAMENTAL RHYTHM PATTERNS, CONTINUED

UNIT II: IRREGULAR DIVISION OF THE BEAT

UNIT III: SYNCOPATION

Appendix C

RECOMMENDED SPEECH CUES

Simple meter

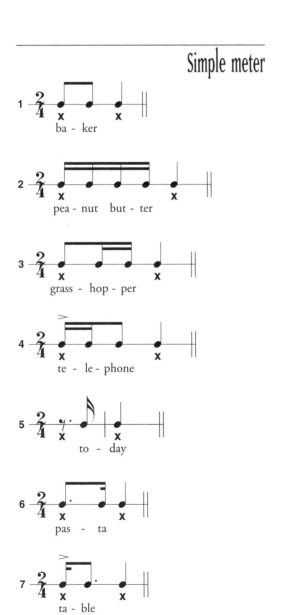

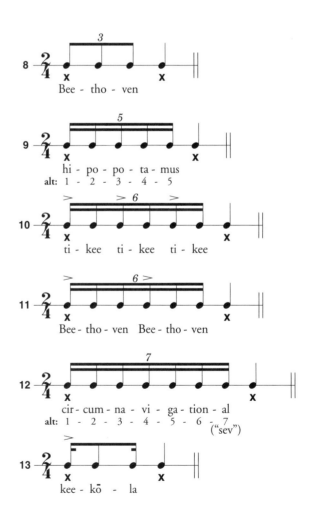

Compound meter

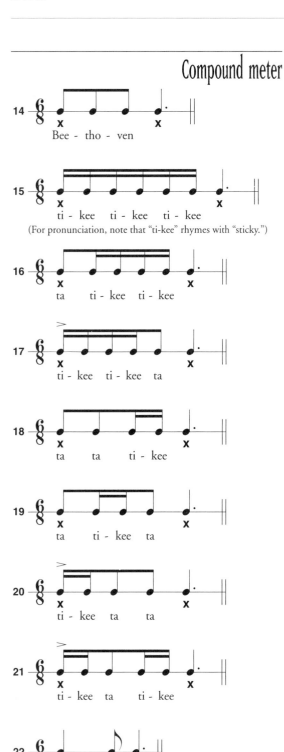

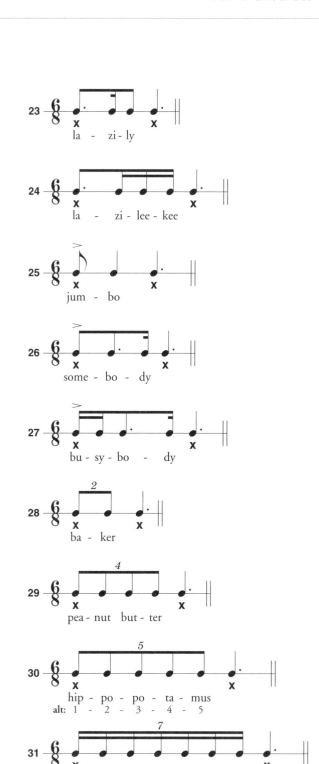

GLOSSARY OF MUSICAL TERMS

8va (ottava) one octave higher than written

a tempo in time; return to the previous tempo

accel. (accelerando) gradually faster

adagio slow (literally, "at ease")

alla napolitana in the style of a genre of sixteenth-century Italian song that originated in Naples

allegretto slightly slower than allegro

allegro fast

allemande a dance common in Baroque dance suites (in $\frac{4}{4}$, moderate tempo)

andante walking tempo (faster than adagio)

animado animated, lively

animé animated, lively

capriccioso capriciously

cédez slow down

con brio with vigor

con fuoco with fire

con impeto impetuously

corda string (for a string instrument, indicates on which string to play)

corrente an Italian dance common in Baroque dance suites (faster than the French *courante*)

cresc. (crescendo) gradually louder

decresc. (decrescendo) gradually softer

dim. (diminuendo) gradually softer

dolce sweet

espr.; espress. (espressivo) with expression

expressif with expression

fantastico fantastic, fanciful

flessibile flexible (rhythmically)

gewichtig heavy

gliss. (glissando) sliding from one pitch to another

langsam slow

larghetto slightly faster than largo

leggiero light

lento slow (slower than adagio)

loco perform at the octave written (after 8*va*)

maestoso majestically

marc. (marcato) marked, with emphasis

marsch march

meno less

moderato moderate tempo (faster than andante)

molto very, much

mouvement tempo

movement de habanera tempo of a habanera (a Cuban dance in $\frac{2}{4}$ meter)

niente nothing

non not

più more

pizz. (pizzicato) plucked rather than bowed (on a violin, viola, cello, or bass)

poco a poco little by little

presto very fast

rit.; ritard. (ritardando) gradually slower

scherz. (scherzando) playful

sempre always, throughout

sim. (simile) similarly (perform as in the preceding measure or passage)

souple et animé supple (flexible) and animated

stacc. (staccato) reduce the duration of a note (e.g., perform ♩ as ♪᷄; also
     indicated as ♩̣ or ♩̭)

stridente strident, rough

sub. (subito) suddenly

sulla tastiera over the fingerboard (on a string instrument, place the bow over
     the fingerboard)

tempo the speed of a composition

tempo di marcia march tempo

tempo giusto strict tempo

ten. (tenuto) held, sustained; legato

tranquille tranquil, quiet, calm

tratt. (trattenuto) held back

vivace lively, quick

Acknowledgments

Adams, *The Chairman Dances* (p. 215): Copyright © 1985 by Associated Music Publishers, Inc. (BMI). International Copyright Secured. All Rights Reserved. Used by Permission.

Bartók, *Concerto for Orchestra* (pp. 206, 207): © Copyright 1946 by Hawkes & Son (London) Ltd; Copyright Renewed. Used by permission of Boosey & Hawkes, Inc.

Bartók, *Music for Strings, Percussion, and Celeste* (p. 196): © Copyright 1937 by Universal Edition; Copyright Renewed. Copyright and Renewal assigned to Boosey & Hawkes, Inc., for the USA. Used by permission of Boosey & Hawkes, Inc.

Bartók, *String Quartet No. 2, Op. 17* (p. 213): Copyright © 1920 (Renewed) by Boosey & Hawkes, Inc.

Berio, *Sequenza I Per Flauto Solo* (p. 214): © Proprieta per tutto il mondo: Edizioni Suvini Zerboni. All Rights Reserved. Used by kind permission of European American Music Distributors Corporation, sole U.S. and Canadian agent for Universal Edition A.G., Vienna, and with kind permission of Edizioni Suvini Zerboni.

Bernstein, "America" from *West Side Story* (p. 209): Copyright © 1956, 1957 (Renewed) by Leonard Bernstein and Stephen Sondheim. The Leonard Bernstein Music Publishing Company, LLC, U.S. and Canadian Publisher. G. Schirmer, Inc., Worldwide print rights and publisher for the rest of the World. International Copyright Secured. All Rights Reserved.

Bernstein, *Fancy Free* (p. 187): Copyright © 1968 by Boosey & Hawkes, Inc.

Bernstein, *Jeremiah* Symphony (p. 193): Copyright © 1963 by Boosey & Hawkes, Inc.

Bernstein, *Trouble in Tahiti* (pp. 194, 196): Copyright © 1953 (Renewed) by Boosey & Hawkes, Inc.

Carter, "Canaries" from *Eight Pieces for Four Timpani* (p. 211): Copyright © 1968 by Associated Music Publishers, Inc. (BMI). International Copyright Secured. All Rights Reserved. Used by Permission.

Carter, *String Quartet No. 1* (pp. 192, 211): Copyright © 1955 (Renewed) by Associated Music Publishers, Inc. (BMI). International Copyright Secured. All Rights Reserved. Used by Permission.

Carter, *String Quartet No. 2* (p. 199): Copyright © 1961 (Renewed) by Associated Music Publishers, Inc. (BMI). International Copyright Secured. All Rights Reserved. Used by Permission.

Copland, *El Salon Mexico* (p. 208): © Copyright 1939 by The Aaron Copland Fund for Music, Inc.; Copyright Renewed. Used by permission of Boosey & Hawkes, Inc., Sole Licensee.

Copland, *Vitebesk* (p. 198): © Copyright 1934 by The Aaron Copland Fund for Music, Inc.; Copyright Renewed. Used by permission of Boosey & Hawkes, Inc., Sole Licensee.

Creston, Symphony No. 2, Op. 35 (p. 194): Copyright © 1954 (Renewed) by G. Schirmer, Inc. (ASCAP). International Copyright Secured. All Rights Reserved. Used by Permission.

Dallapiccola, *Il Prigioniero* (p. 207): Reprinted by permission of Edizioni Suvini Zerboni, Milan, Italy.

Dallapiccola, *Sex Carmina Alcaei* (p. 213): Reprinted by permission of Edizioni Suvini Zerboni, Milan, Italy.

Gershwin, *I Got Rhythm* (p. vii): © 1930 (Renewed) WB Music Corp. All Rights Reserved. Used by Permission. WARNER BROS. PUBLICATIONS U.S. INC., Miami, FL 33014.

Hindemith, *Die Harmonie der Welt* (p. 197): © Schott & Co. Ltd., London, 1952 © renewed. All Rights Reserved. Used by permission of European American Music Distributors Corporation, sole U.S. and Canadian agent for Schott & Co. Ltd., London.

Ives, *The Cage* (p. 214): Copyright © 1955 by Peer International Corporation. International Copyright Secured. Printed in USA. All Rights Reserved. Used by Permission.

Ives, Symphony No. 4 (p. 197): Copyright © 1965 (Renewed) by Associated Music Publishers, Inc. (BMI). International Copyright Secured. All Rights Reserved. Used by Permission.

Milhaud, *Le boeuf sur le toit* (p. 189): Used by permission of Associated Music Publishers, Inc. (BMI).

Milhaud, *La création du monde* (p. 190): Copyright © 1929 (Renewed) by Associated Music Publishers, Inc. (BMI). International Copyright Secured. Used by Permission.

Milhaud, *Saudades Do Brazil* (p. 186): Copyright © 1922 (Renewed) by Associated Music Publishers, Inc. (BMI).

International Copyright Secured. All Rights Reserved. Used by Permission.

Milhaud, *Symphonic Suite No. 2* (p. 205): Copyright © 1921 (Renewed) by Associated Music Publishers, Inc. (BMI). International Copyright Secured. All Rights Reserved. Used by Permission.

Orff, *Carmina Burana* (p. 210): © 1937 B. Schott's Soehne. © renewed. All Rights Reserved. Used by permission of European American Music Distributors Corporation, sole U.S. and Canadian agent for B. Schott's Soehne.

Ravel, *Alborada Del Gracioso* (p. 157): Used by Permission of G. Schirmer, Inc. (ASCAP).

Ravel, *Rapsodie Espagnole* (p. 112): Used by Permission of G. Schirmer, Inc. (ASCAP).

Ravel, *Sheherazade* (p. 113): Used by Permission of G. Schirmer, Inc. (ASCAP).

Reich, *Clapping Music for Two Performers* (p. 214): © Copyright 1980 by Universal Edition (London) Ltd., London. All Rights Reserved. Used by permission of European American Music Distributors Corporation, sole U.S. and Canadian agent for Universal Edition (London) Ltd., London.

Schuman, *Symphony for Strings* (p. 188): Copyright © 1943 (Renewed) by Associated Music Publishers, Inc. (BMI). International Copyright Secured. All Rights Reserved. Used by Permission.

Stravinsky, *Rhythm and motion* (p. vii): from *An Encyclopedia of Quotations about Music,* edited by Nat Shapiro. New York: Doubleday, 1978, p. 39.

Stravinsky, *L'histoire du soldat* (p. 208): Copyright © 1924 (Renewed) by J & W Chester (England). All rights for the U.S. and Canada controlled by Edition Wilhelm Hansen/Chester Music New York, Inc. (ASCAP). International Copyright Secured. All Rights Reserved. Used by Permission.

Stravinsky, *Petrushka* (pp. 112, 188): © Copyright by Edition Russe de Musique. Copyright assigned to Boosey & Hawkes, Inc. Reserved Edition. © Copyright 1947, 1948 by Boosey & Hawkes, Inc., Copyright Renewed. Used by permission.

Stravinsky, *Rite of Spring* (pp. 186, 207): © Copyright 1921 by Edition Russe de Musique. Copyright assigned to Boosey & Hawkes, Inc. for the world. Used by permission.

Varèse, *Density 21.5* (p. 198): Reprinted by permission of Hendon Music, Inc., Agents for Casa Ricordi/BMG Ricordi, Copyright Owner and Publisher.

Varèse, *Ionisation* (p. 197): Reprinted by permission of Boosey & Hawkes, Inc.

Villa-Lobos, *Bachianas Brasileiras No. 5* (p. 202): Copyright © 1954 (Renewed) by Associated Music Publishers, Inc. (BMI). International Copyright Secured. All Rights Reserved. Used by Permission.

Villa-Lobos, *Canções tipicas brasileiros, "Xango"* (p. 195): © 1929 Editions Max Eschig. Used By Permission Of The Publisher. Sole Representative U.S.A. Theodore Presser Company.

Walton, *Violin Concerto* (p. 194): © 1945, Oxford University Press. Reproduced by permission.

Webern, *Five Canons,* Op. 16, No. 3 (p. 198): Copyright 1928 by Universal Edition. Copyright renewed. All Rights Reserved. Used by permission of European American Music Distributors Corporation, sole U.S. and Canadian agent for Universal Edition.

Wuorinen, *Bicinium for Two Oboes* (p. 210): © 1971. Used by permission of C. F. Peters Corporation.

INDEX

C 16, 70

¢ 70

♪ = ♪ 95

⁒ 38

accent 143, 144

agogic accent 144

alla breve 70

ametric music 213

anacrusis 44

augmentation canon 54

augmentation dot 13

beaming 15

beaming over rests 37

beat unit 8

borrowed division 112

breve 69, 210

canon 23

canon cancrizans 39

common time 16

composite meter 19, 203

compound meter 3, 28

conducting 2

   one beat per measure 36

   two beats per measure 12

   three beats per measure 13

   four beats per measure 10

   five beats per measure (2 + 3; 3 + 2) 19

   seven beats per measure (4 + 3; 3 + 4) 19

crab canon 39

cross rhythms 148

cut time 70

diminution canon 77

division unit 28

double-dotted note 49

double meter 208

double whole note 69

double whole rest 69

duple meter 9, 12

duplet 128

dynamic accent 144

echoing xix

embellished accent 144

half rest 11

harmonic accent 144

hemiola 156

hocket 23

hypermeasure 75

hypermeter 74, 86

ictus 2

inverted dotting 48

irregular division of the beat 111, 127

   with measured tremolo 118

longa 210

measured tremolo 50, 62

meter 7

meter changes 18

metric modulation 210

multi-measure rests 45

note endings 11

pattern accent 144

pickup 44
pitch accent 144
polymetric music 212
practicing 1
quadruple meter 9, 10
quadruplet 129
quarter note 11
quarter rest 11
quintuplet 114, 130
recommended listening: simple meter, compound
    meter; quadruple meter, duple meter, triple
    meter; composite meter (2 + 3; 3 + 2) 26
recommended listening: syncopation 155
retrograde canon 39
rhythm cells xvii, 1, 11
    in simple meter 219
    in compound meter 220
rhythmic alteration in Baroque music 189
Scotch snap 48
septuplet 118, 131
sextolet 115
sextuplet 115

simple meter 7
speech cue method xviii, 15
speech cues
    in simple meter 221
    in compound meter 222
split measures 63
superduplet 148
supertriplet 149
syncopation 143
tempo 3
tempo modulation 210
tie 11
time signature 7, 8
tremolo 50, 62
triple meter 9, 13
triplet 113
unmeasured tremolo 51
unusual beat units 209
upbeat 44
whole-measure rest 18
whole-note rest 14